Nature Abhors a Vacuum

A Handbook for the Domestically Impaired

Kathryn Hammer

D1417040

CB

CONTEMPORARY
BOOKS

CHICAGO

Library of Congress Cataloging-in-Publication Data

Hammer, Kathryn.
    Nature abhors a vacuum / Kathryn Hammer.
       p.   cm.
    ISBN 0-8092-3631-1 (pbk.)
    1. Home economics—Humor.   I. Title.
  TX295.H24   1994
  640'.207—dc20   94-19174
                                CIP

Published by Contemporary Books, Inc.
Two Prudential Plaza, Chicago, Illinois 60601-6790
Manufactured in the United States of America
International Standard Book Number: 0-8092-3631-1
10   9   8   7   6   5   4   3

To Jon and Nick, who decorate our home
with love and laughter, bringing immeasurable joy
and beauty to wet towels,
muddy sneakers, and dirty dishes.

Contents

Acknowledgments

No author writes in a vacuum. *About* vacuums, maybe, but never *in* them. So a grateful nod of the upholstery attachment goes to my editor, Linda Gray; my agent, Nancy Yost; the Housewife Writers on Prodigy for friendship, advice, and frog spit; and members of the Indiana Writers' Workshop, who know that one dust jacket makes up for a thousand dust bunnies.

Other (unwitting) accomplices in research for this book were college roomies; my Perfect Neighbor Connie with the Perfect House who always has everything I need to borrow; my phone-friend Laura, patron saint of laughter; Anita, who aids and abets in fun-filled hours of task avoidance; French, just because; Diane, Clarke, Mark, and Jim, who expanded my definition of what can be put into a kitchen freezer; terrific in-laws who never criticize; and the coffee growers of Colombia who, with the world's finest chocolatiers, stood loyally by my side throughout the writing process.

Finally, to Mom and Dad who passed on to me a light heart and love of family, if not their tidiness genes: See, I *told* you a messy room was a sign of creativity!

Introduction
Why You Need This Book

Perhaps you had a suspicion that you might be Different—not like the Others. At first you tried not to notice the subtle signs: the snide looks, the whispered comments, the gift-wrapped bottle of Lysol in your mailbox.

Your children started coming home with reports of playing in homes containing strange items called *bedspreads* and *coasters*.

In your own visits to the homes of neighbors, you noticed the odd way in which you could pick up your feet without resistance from the kitchen floor.

Eventually, it all came together, and *you knew*. You were Domestically Impaired. You searched around for a clean surface on which to throw yourself and have a good cry. Realizing there was none, you resigned yourself to a life of despair with your crippling disability.

1

Well, it's time you stopped feeling like the worthless scum that covers your shower stall!

So what if your neighbor's contour sheets are neatly folded in flat, tidy stacks in her perfumed linen closet while yours are wadded up in a ball like the aftermath of a toga party?

(The ability to fold a contour sheet is, in itself, an Unnatural Act and should be punishable by law under the same statutes governing romantic encounters with farm animals.)

This perfect homemaker fetish all started one day when an anal-retentive mama's-boy psychologist named Stanley wrote too many prescriptions for himself and decided that one's home is an extension of one's personality—an infallible statement to the world of who you are and how you wish to be viewed. This theory caught on among other psychologists, as it fit their criteria for being totally subjective and unprovable. Besides, *they* have full-time housekeepers and reside in magnificent homes decorated by people named Serge.

(These same psychologists will also be happy to handle your therapy to overcome the depression that results from knowing that your personality can be described in terms of soap scum and mildew.)

The notion that the way you keep house is a reflection of your soul is, of course, patently absurd. Your home has no shiny surfaces capable of reflecting *anything*, much less your soul. But if the state of one's home is indeed a reflection of personality, what does your home say about you? Does it speak of a woman of grace and charm, serenity and order? Of course not!

Your house should be bound and gagged. It has no business talking behind your back, spilling its guts on what it knows about you—or worse, screaming obscenities at innocent passersby. Face it . . . your house is the brick and stucco version of Tourette's syndrome.

Your home is telling anyone who will listen that you are Domestically Impaired. But be of good cheer! You are not alone. In fact, there are millions of domestically impaired people who are much worse than you are, as seen televised nightly on "Cops."

Your ranks, in fact, greatly outnumber the Domestically Gifted—but you'd never know it because the DG Neurotics are far more vocal and militant ("I am woman, hear me vacuum!"). They only *seem* to be the norm because they hog all the space in the women's magazines, thereby inflating perceptions of their numbers. (This is a technique borrowed from Amazonian rain-forest frogs who puff themselves up to grotesque proportions to intimidate *National Geographic* photographers.)

It's time for you to hold your head up proudly, look through the haze in the mirror, and say, "I am Domestically Impaired and I don't care who knows it!"

So brush the Cheez-Ohs off the sofa, find the coffee table, put your feet up, and prepare to regain your self-esteem.

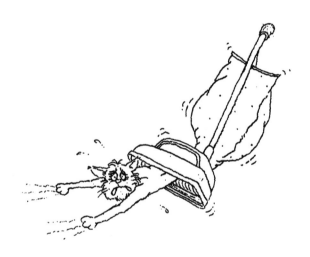

1
Are You Domestically Impaired?
A Scientific Quiz

Of course you are! Why else would you be holding this book in your hands? Would you find Dick Cavett browsing remedial reading primers? Does Rush Limbaugh curl up with *Ms.* magazine?

Admit it. You thought the Good Housekeeping Seal was a fastidious aquatic mammal with a dust fetish, didn't you?

Besides, if you were not Domestically Impaired, you would be too *busy* to read this book. You would be bustling about vacuuming your refrigerator coils and ironing your garbage-bag twist ties. You would be gleefully crocheting throw rugs out of styrofoam packing peanuts, disinfecting household objects with impunity, and otherwise frittering away your life while driving your family and friends completely bonkers.

But just in case you're not quite sure about your domestic orientation, the following quiz will help to

5

determine if you are genuinely Domestically Impaired or if you are just going through a rebellious phase:

1. *On the bottle of a popular cleaning liquid, there is a portrait of a large bald person wearing one earring. What is this product?*

The correct answer is Mr. Clean. If you thought it was a hair restoration product called Mr. Chemotherapy, score 3 points. Give yourself 5 points if you said it was Sinéad O'Connor's revolutionary new fragrance called Angry Obsession.

2. *What is the best method to use when attempting to wash a sinkful of dishes with dried-on egg?*

You are Domestically Gifted if you knew that you should soak the dishes in cold water. Give yourself 2 points if you would have used any of the following: sandblaster, blowtorch, muriatic acid. Score 3 points if you said you would put the dishes on the floor for the dog to lick clean, and 5 points if you asked, "What's a sink?"

3. *If you were out of window cleaner, what item from your kitchen pantry could you use to shine your mirrors?*

This is a tricky one. Minute Maid or Aunt Jemima *sound* like reasonable answers, but neither of these ladies does windows. If you said vinegar, go to the head of the class. Score 5 points if you said Miracle Whip or I Can't Believe It's Not Butter!

4. *What is the best way to prevent waxy yellow buildup on your kitchen floor?*

Give yourself 2 points if you answered, "Don't use yellow wax," and 4 points if you thought it was a good idea to maintain a protective film of kitchen gunk. The high-scoring 6-point answer is, of course, to avoid cleaning your ears in the kitchen.

5. *What is meant by "putting up preserves"?*

Score 4 points if you thought this involved a Marlin Perkins wildlife habitat project, and 5 points if you said it had something to do with hanging marmalade on the curtain rods.

6. *What is the best way to eliminate kitchen odors?*

Installing an exhaust fan and simmering a pot of vanilla extract on the stove are both good, albeit unimaginative, answers. Chalk up 2 points if you said, "Quit cooking roadkill and empty the garbage more than once a year," and 5 points if you suggested basting the chicken wings with Mennen Speed Stick.

7. *What is the proper method for eliminating bloodstains on clothing?*

The Domestically Gifted would know that meat tenderizer and a cold-water soak will do the trick. Score 5 points if you said, "Switch to a higher absorbency pad."

8. *What is the function of an item called a plumber's helper?*

It is, of course, a plunger used to unclog toilets and drains. Give yourself 5 points if you thought a plumber's helper was a boxed casserole dinner containing dried prunes and Metamucil.

9. *What is the best way to control dust bunnies?*

The Domestically Neurotic would, predictably, suggest dusting. Score a full 10 points if you thought it would be helpful to place casserole dishes of d-Con under the bed.

10. *When doing laundry, what is the best method for sorting clothes?*

The conventional wisdom is to separate lights from darks, and fine washables, such as silk, from things like Velcro and S.O.S. soap pads. However, give yourself 3 points if you think that separating laundry is discriminatory, racist, or homophobic.

Scoring. 0–10: You're obviously a spy for the Heloise Fan Club or a Stepford Wife or both. Leave quietly and no one will get hurt.

11–25: You have a little too much knowledge to be classified as Domestically Impaired, but you are sufficiently flawed to be welcomed in most circles.

26–45: You are definitely Impaired and are undoubtedly loved by all your friends, if not your mother-in-law.

46–55: Have you considered the exciting career opportunities available to you in the glamorous field of Third World Interior Design?

2
Housekeeping Fanatics
Recognizing the Enemy

THE NEW WORLD ORDERLINESS
PREPARING FOR THE POLITICAL ASYLUM

Millions of Domestically Impaired individuals are unaware of the growing threat to their casual lifestyle. As their happy, well-adjusted children frolic about in mountains of dirty laundry, world leaders further their chilling agenda.

The Domestically Gifted fanatics control the publishing business and the broadcast media. (When was the last time you saw a magazine called *Really Average Homes and Gardens* or *So-So Housekeeping?*)

Insidious, subliminal propaganda turns up everywhere. TV anchorpeople routinely segue their news stories with the phrase, "On the domestic scene . . ." Presidents continually stress the need to address "domestic issues." They spend their days *ironing out* problems, dealing with *pressing* matters, and making *sweeping* decisions on the House floor.

It is patently obvious that this is a conspiracy, a

sort of Four-Bedroom-Tri-Level Commission, headed up by such subversives as Heloise, Martha Stewart, Mary Ellen, and, yes, every president this country has ever had. (Ever wonder *why* it's called the White House?)

So you can see why it is so important to be able to identify these people and to make the distinction between housekeeping fanatics, who think there are dust bunnies under every bed, and rational people like you, who KNOW there are dust bunnies under every bed but don't give a damn.

SPOTTING THE
DOMESTICALLY GIFTED IN THE WILD

Like all subversives trained to infiltrate and assimilate into the community, the Domestically Gifted fanatics will attempt to look and act like you. However, it is easy to spot them—they look very much like you and other normal people in the same way that Cindy Crawford and Tom Cruise look like average people. The basic parts are the same—they're just assembled differently.

You can pick out the Domestically Gifted in a crowd—if you would want to, which you probably wouldn't unless you're easily amused and bored out of your skull.

Telltale signs:

• Looks like Sue Ann Nivens (You look like David Niven in drag.)

• Flushed face from baking snickerdoodles (You got your flushed face in the tanning bed or from reading the steamy parts of romance novels.)

- Her fragrance is a subtle blend of Pine Sol, fabric softener, and Similac (Your fragrance is the perfumed insert that came in the department store bill.)

- Wears an ankle-length denim dropped-waist jumper and a blouse with a neatly pressed Peter Pan collar (You wear sweats smeared with Peter Pan peanut butter.)

- Does needlepoint or knitting while waiting in line (You amuse yourself by very carefully plucking out a single hair from the head of the person in front of you and then glaring at him when he turns around.)

- Carries Kleenex and moist towelettes in her purse (You can't find your purse.)

- Drives a station wagon or minivan with a sign in the window saying Baby on Board and a bumper sticker proclaiming that the driver of the car is the Proud Parent of a Straight-A Student (You drive a Land Rover with a bumper sticker that says, "My Child Was Acquitted!")

- Carries the latest issue of *Parenting, Family Circle,* or *Refunding Gazette* (You have the magazines-on-tape versions of *Cosmopolitan* and *Playgirl.*)

THE AT-HOME BEHAVIORAL PATTERNS OF THE SPECIES

The distinction between the Domestically Gifted and the Domestically Impaired is never so obvious as it is at home. Only those clearly out of touch (such as presidential advisors and the people who bag your groceries with the tomatoes on the bottom) would not notice these subtle differences: (DG = Domestically Gifted; DI = Domestically Impaired)

DG: Covers all her cookbooks with Con-Tact paper to match her kitchen decor.

DI: Thinks Con-Tact paper is the outer wrapping on a decongestant box.

***

DG: Files her recipes, written in calligraphy on 3 × 5 cards, in a gaily decorated recipe box.

DI: Files her recipes, cut from the back of cereal boxes and mushroom soup cans, in an empty Pampers carton in the garage.

***

DG: Stores all her leftovers in see-through, stackable plastic containers in the fridge, so she can see at a glance what she has and can make use of the items at each meal.

DI: Stores her leftovers in wadded tinfoil and empty margarine tubs so she can see at a glance that there is nothing to eat and must therefore send out for Chinese.

***

DG: Has all her snapshots in one place—organized, labeled, and in albums, with the negatives in their plastic sleeves tucked in the back.

DI: Has all her rolls of undeveloped film from the past two decades safely stored in seven strategic locations someplace somewhere, near as she can remember.

***

DG: Consolidates half-empty condiment jars to conserve on refrigerator space and ensure timely usage of the product.

DI: Keeps three partial jars of watery pickle relish, two bottles of very old mustard whose contents resemble the surface of the moon, and four crusted-shut Miracle Whip jars as decoys to dissuade family members from between-meal snacks.

***

DG: Arranges perishable food items by expiration date in the fridge.

DI: Uses the scratch-and-sniff method of determining freshness, along with the time-tested technique of handing a suspect container of indeterminate origin to a child and saying, "Here. Taste this."

***

DG: Has placed all hazardous cleaning products on a top shelf, each marked with a Mr. Yuk sticker.

DI: Has no cleaning products except for inoperable aerosol cans with clogged nozzles. Her children have placed the Mr. Yuk stickers on all the foil-covered casserole dishes in the fridge.

***

DG: Writes all her Christmas cards while on summer vacation, stamps them, and files them for December mailings.

DI: Writes all her Christmas cards after she sees who sent cards to her.

***

DG: Has all her children's inoculation records, birth certificates, and report cards organized and catalogued where she can put her finger on them instantly as the need arises.

DI: Has all her children's inoculation records, birth certificates, and report cards. Somewhere. If the need arises, she can produce said documents in two weeks or less, along with her prom corsage, a Partridge Family lunch box, and three unopened electric bills from a previous residence, while at the same time solving the mystery of the strange disappearance of two gerbils in August 1987.

***

DG: Her strings of Christmas lights are neatly repacked in their original boxes and stored in the attic in a labeled, waterproof stacking tub.

DI: Her children used the Christmas lights to hog-tie the baby-sitter in the attic.

***

DG: Kitchen floors gleam like the mirrored surface of a placid harbor.

DI: Kitchen floors resemble Boston Harbor.

ARE YOU IN DANGER
OF BECOMING ONE OF THEM?

THE EIGHT WARNING SIGNS OF
HYPERDOMESTICITY

Certain household practices are warning signals of a dangerous hormonal imbalance called Hyperdomesticity. Initially, the condition is marked by seemingly innocuous behavior, such as trying on aprons ("just for fun") and playing fairy godmother with the toilet-bowl brush. Words like *whiter, brighter, new,* and *improved* start creeping into the vocabulary.

Later stages are marked by recurrent fantasies about the tid-D-Bol man and increasingly callous disrespect for one's own time, such as making your own paper towels by washing, bleaching, and drying the book review section of the *New York Times.*

The following signals should be viewed with grave concern:

• Do you wash and dry coffee filters for reuse?

• Do you make your own rubber bands from old rubber gloves?

• Do you clean the can opener blade after each use?

• Do you have an 8 × 10 glossy of Heloise over your sink?

• Do you spend your leisure time in Target's housewares department fingering kitchen gadgets?

• Did you celebrate your last wedding anniversary with a Tupperware party?

• Is the scent of Lysol a turn-on?

DISPELLING THE MYTHS

In order to start feeling good about yourself again, you need to recognize the myths about housekeeping. Here are a few of the more popular myths circulating about the Domestically Impaired.

MYTH: Your inability to achieve orgasm with the vacuum cleaner attachments is a sexual dysfunction.

TRUTH: If vacuuming were a natural, basic urge, pre-historic women would have owned mastodons named Kirby and dragged them around the cave by their trunks. Of course, we know this did not happen, because if it had, Leonard Nimoy would have narrated a scientific documentary on the subject called "In Search of Dust Bunnies."

MYTH: Unless you cook from scratch, you are a lazy, good-for-nothing slattern with no regard for the well-being of your family's nutritional needs.

TRUTH: It is a precious jewel of a mother who recognizes her own limitations. The reason your family is still alive today probably has a lot to do with the fact that you *don't* cook from scratch. Your concern for the comfort and safety of their lower intestinal tracts is ample proof of your love.

MYTH: Nondomestic types go against nature; being a homemaker and creating a cozy, orderly home is part of a primal "nesting instinct" and is a feminine biological need.

TRUTH: There's a cross-species double standard at work here. Birds and rodents are allowed to demonstrate their nesting instinct by considering bits of lint, string, twigs, and shredded newspaper to be highly attractive Home Decor. Apparently, keeping *your* nest knee-deep in the same stuff doesn't count. Face it, if housekeeping were a biological instinct, women would have evolved with upholstery attachments on their uteruses, and estrogen would remove ground-in dirt.

3
Housekeeping Strategies
A Smorgasbord of Options
for the Domestically Starved

THE LEONA HELMSLEY METHOD

The world's best-kept homes and prison cells are owned by enormously wealthy people with a staff of full-time uniformed servants. This is an excellent strategy if you have a substantial family fortune.

THE SIEGFRIED AND ROY METHOD

If the only uniformed person you can afford to have hanging around your house is the Orkin man, consider another housekeeping strategy: the Art of Illusion. It is no coincidence that Siegfried and Roy and David Copperfield have very clean homes.

Of course, the average person does not have holograms at her disposal, so she must rely on Misdirection. This is a technique used by magicians when they want you to *think* they've done something when they haven't (or, in the case of congressmen, vice versa). It is also called Being Led Down the Garden Path.

For example, imagine a magician (or a senator) wants you to think that there's a tiger in the box with his scantily clad assistant. The box will rock violently, there will be sounds of savage roaring, perhaps even some tiger droppings lying about. But, of course, the assistant is in the green room sipping Diet Coke and reading *Elle*, and the tiger is heavily sedated in the back of a semi.

You can keep house the same way. Of course, a really, really good illusion costs big money. But if you can save up enough for just one large albino tiger to roam about your house, you can be sure no one will notice the coffee-cup rings atop the toilet tank.

In the meantime, you can work on honing the fine art of Illusion and Misdirection in a more modest fashion. Here is a sample technique:

Fill an atomizer or spritz bottle with a household disinfectant characterized by a strong, identifiable scent. Pine, lemon, and dental office are good choices. Now spray every lightbulb in the house. Let dry. Fifteen minutes before your family or guests arrive, turn on all the lights, stand back, and wait for the compliments.

Variation: If you want to elicit sympathy, slather the bulbs with Vicks VapoRub and sniff a lot. People will assume that your home is a mammoth pigsty because you are too sick to clean. *Bonus:* Visitors will leave quickly.

THE SMITHSONIAN–OLD MONEY–
ECCENTRIC METHOD

No need to excavate through the junk and clutter when said junk and clutter can merely be renamed

"Antiques & Collectibles." Even Domestic Neurotics approve of dusty, water-stained stuff that has been collected from the four corners of the world over several generations by wildly outrageous and colorful relatives with names such as Uncle Montague and Cousin Wilhelmina Runnymeade of the Tudor side of the family. (Never mind that you *have* no Uncle Montague. You may feel free to make up all this stuff, since the only people who are conversant in matters of lineage are busy clutching their buzzers on "Jeopardy.")

The success of this method hinges on your skill in conveying an ambience of Museum Quality to the dustatorium you call your living room. Rope off areas with red velvet cording attached to brass standards, and speak in reverent, docent-type tones when leading visitors through the area: "This room is exactly as it was when Cornwallis received notice of Mussolini's surrender in the Crimean War. That stain on the carpeting was where Vasco da Gama stood with his muddy boots, and of course, that Dracula plastic tumbler stuck to the TV tray was used by Bram Stoker himself the night he and Winston Churchill raped Great Aunt Clarice. Those are Churchill's cigar ashes on the LA-Z-Boy."

THE MAHATMA GANDHI/KWAI CHANG CAINE METHOD

Divesting yourself of all material possessions frees you from the need to clean those things. You must take care to maintain a public posture of great spiritual enlightenment, lest people assume you've simply had everything repossessed by the finance company. So you must walk around saying very wise things. For example, when someone asks you why you have no furniture in your home, you gaze into the distance and say haltingly (so as to sound wise and Oriental like David Carradine), "Of what need . . . do mountains have . . . of the water lily's nectar?" *Warning:* This is not real effective when you've got Guns 'N Roses blaring in the background and the TV is tuned to "Beavis and Butt-Head."

THE HEART OF GOLD, SALT OF THE EARTH METHOD

This method of keeping house not only gets you off the hook for normal standards of household hygiene, but lays a guilt trip on anyone who does adhere to them. The key here is to fill your house with everyone else's kids. Encourage them to call you Mom. Supplement with a menagerie of stray animals that would surely have been gassed by the Humane Society had you not taken them in.

If you can stay sane with all the noise and chaos, you've got a built-in excuse for the condition of your house. You can whisper sad little stories to visitors, such as, "It's such a shame . . . so many of these children aren't allowed to play at home because their mothers are too concerned about a clean home. Can you imagine?"

ASSORTED DIVERSIONARY TACTICS

• Upscale magazines with names such as *Town and Country, Better Homes and Gardens,* and *Snob* are available for pennies at library sales and garage sales. Pile these liberally around your home, preferably into big wicker baskets on top of last week's laundry, which you then set on top of the huge pet stain next to the couch.

• Accumulate an array of discontinued fabric samples and lay them out over your furniture. This gives the impression that you are in the midst of redecorating your entire house, and all disarray is summarily excused.

• Keep a large scrub bucket and mop in the front hall, along with a rubber band and large workshirt. When the doorbell rings, quickly pull your hair back in the rubber band, toss on the workshirt, and lean against the mop handle while explaining through the screen door that it's been almost two days since the floor's been disinfected, and you simply cannot let it go any longer.

• Keep a large supply of your child's artwork handy to slap over dirty refrigerator fronts and finger-marked doors. If you do not have a child, you may make your own. (Art, that is. Not children. The making of children is somewhat more involved.) Using a dull crayon held in your nondominant hand, quickly sketch out a Picassoesque rendition of a bowl of spaghetti.

• For those times when it's just too much trouble to scrape the oatmeal or pizza off the wall, hang a picture frame around the offending area. This is most effective if you've had the foresight to attach an engraved plate to the frame saying "Andy Warhol."

• After returning from the laundry with your husband's shirts, remove plastic and tags. Set up the ironing board and hang shirts in the doorway. Close off the air conditioning vents in that room, close the door, and go read a book. When you hear the little man's car pulling into the driveway, dampen your hair and your blouse, and take up position behind the iron.

• Beds unmade and visitors walking in the door? Stripping them is lots faster, and the pile of sheets on the floor gives the impression you were just about to Actually Launder.

• Keep a large supply of canning jars handy for days when you want to be left alone. Line them up on the counter, drag out a large stockpot, and announce cheerily, "Anyone want to help?" The family will scatter like cockroaches. (*Note:* Do not, under any circumstances, *actually* can!)

4
Cleaning
The Womanly Art of Performing Thankless Chores for Free

TALKING DIRTY:
CLEAN UP YOUR GRAMMAR

Clean is good. Cleaning is not.

Cleaning, you see, is a verb and, as such, requires action. Of course, *sleeping, shopping,* and *sipping margaritas* are also verbs, but they are passive verbs, and therefore good verbs.

The verb *to clean* is conjugated as follows: "I clean, you clean, she cleans, we clean, y'all clean, they clean." The first person form of the verb is the common usage, and the masculine form of the third person singular "he cleans" is almost never seen. Your job is to revive the second and third person usage, and to make first person obsolete.

The majority of household advice relates to cleaning: what to clean, how to clean it, different ways to clean it, the cheapest way to clean it, when to clean it, what to wear while cleaning it, and blah blah blah, *ad pukum.*

23

The only subjects never addressed are: 1) alternatives to cleaning it and 2) *why* it needs to be cleaned at all. Actually, these are the only two questions that matter—and with practice, you'll learn how to make up exceptionally convoluted answers such as the kind used in Senate subcommittee hearings.

WHY DOES IT NEED TO BE CLEANED AT ALL?

Before beginning any cleaning project, ask yourself the following questions:

Q. *Will the world be a better place if we can eat off of [fill in the blank]? Would we* want *to eat off of it?*

A. Of course not. Most civilized people do not eat from toilets or lap tapioca from the linoleum. So unless the item you are contemplating is a plate, the answer is no.

Q. *Will anyone notice if [fill in the blank] is no longer encrusted in grease and carbon?*

A. Depends on the ages of your kids. If they were born after you last cleaned it, chances are they'll assume the item has disappeared, having been replaced by a foreign, shiny object of suspect origin. Your efforts should be redirected to something that will get you the proper recognition, such as borrowing Rice Krispie treats from your neighbor.

Q. *Is this the best use of my time at the moment? Would it* ever *be the best use of my time?*

A. No. The best use of your time would be in the rain forests of South America, extracting sap from tree bark for cancer cure research. If you can't get to South America, other options include getting a facial or trying on clothes at The Limited.

Q. *If I don't clean it, what will happen?*

A. Usually, the answer is "nothing." There are situations, however, in which the answer is more complicated, such as your billionaire uncle with the dirt fetish stopping by on the way to an appointment with his estate attorney to draw up a new will.

THREE COOL
ALTERNATIVES TO CLEANING

1. Leave it as is. If you live alone and have no visitors, have a reasonably efficient immune system and a strong stomach, cleaning is unnecessary. Your time could be appropriated for more productive pursuits, such as collecting fragrance samples from the cosmetics counters or mutilating Denise Austin exercise videos.

2. Find a new use for it. Items that have become impractical to use due to accumulated filth may be quite serviceable under another guise. For example, grease-encrusted barbecue grill grates may be sprinkled with glitter and presented to your daughter as an accessory for her doll collection. ("Look what Mommy has for you, sweetie! It's B-Girl Barbie's County Lockup!")

3. Burn it and buy a new one. Often the cost of a new item is less than the cumulative cost of cleaning, which includes products, tools, time, and aggravation, not to mention the cost of fingernail repair and expensive trips to the dermatologist to handle that nasty, oozing rash on your hands caused by cleaning chemicals.

SCIENTIFIC, SCHOLARLY REASONS WHY CLEANING IS A BAD IDEA

1. Cleaning kicks up dust that will aggravate your allergies, causing your mucous membranes to react in all sorts of highly unappetizing ways. Naturally, this will adversely affect your love life, leading to divorce and broken families—factors that have been implicated in the rising rate of illiteracy and juvenile crime. Do you want this on your head?

2. Cleaning raises taxes. Many household products upset the delicate ecological balance of nature in a sort of global PMS. (Remember, when Mother Nature's upset, ain't nobody happy.) Cleaning, in fact, entails murdering billions of microscopic food sources for billions of obscure little life forms with unpronounceable names. This will eventually threaten the survival of countless species, necessitating monstrous federal projects in which Al Gore will declare your kitchen a protected wetland, and hundreds of research geeks with pocket protectors will swarm about your house, attempting to look as if they are performing an actual, useful function so they can raise your taxes.

3. Caustic cleaning chemicals are unable to distinguish between harmful bacteria and those helpful Pac-Man microbes with smiley faces that gobble up evil, malevolent, slavering bacteria. (*Note:* This is a simplification for the layperson.) To prove this, scientists at MIT conducted experiments in which Liquid-Plumr was added to yogurt and fed to some really stupid undergraduates. Autopsies showed that the good bacteria in the yogurt was destroyed and the product was rendered inedible—ample proof of the dangers of cleaning products and the hazards of being an undergraduate.

4. Cleaning raises your insurance rates. Most household accidents are caused by carelessness while cleaning. Falls, cuts, scrapes, contusions, abrasions, unsightly welts, and the inhalation of toxic fumes result in costly visits to the emergency room and countless wasted hours filling out insurance forms and trying to communicate with the non-English-speaking staff. By contrast, the statistical probability of being injured while lying on the sofa reading *Cosmopolitan* is negligible.

5. Excessively clean homes can be psychologically and financially disastrous. Sociologists have determined, by spying through peepholes in ladies' restrooms, that the person on the block with the cleanest house is the designated target for malicious gossip and snide speculation regarding obsessive-compulsive, anal-retentive, neurotic behavior. This causes severe depression, necessitating a three-month stay in a designer mental health facility that caters to the families

of sullen teenagers with blue hair, nose studs, and comprehensive health insurance.

WARNINGS BEFORE CLEANING THAT MAY SAVE YOUR LIFE OR SOMETHING

Be aware that cleaning renders many items useless. This is because family members no longer recognize the item once it's cleaned and therefore have no idea what it is or what to use it for, resulting in chaos, disorder, and, often, tragedy.

Case history: Apparently suffering from a severe lack of meaningful goals and the inaccessibility of cable TV, Susie Potter (not her real name) from Morgan, Minnesota, ZIP code 56266, spent an entire afternoon cleaning the blade on the electric can opener. Not recognizing the foreign, shiny new object, her oldest son mistook it for a videotape splicer and single-handedly wiped out the family's entire collection of *Sweatin' to the Oldies.* Susie (not her real name) is now forced to do her aerobics to "Nightline" while imagining Ted Koppel in a tank top and tights.

Many older items are held together by dirt and crud. Because cleaning often entails removal of these adhesive substances, which are needed to keep things from falling apart, cleaning can create safety hazards and great expense.

Case history: Having skipped school on the day Mr. Pitzen was handing out mimeographed sheets on the symbiotic molecular structures of toilet ring caulking and naturally occurring toilet gunk, Molly Z. (not her real name) was blithely unaware of the danger she posed to her family when she walked into the bathroom with her scrub brush. It was only after her once-devoted husband Bob (not his real name) was found pinned beneath the overturned toilet that Molly realized her mistake. Fortunately, subsequent royalties from the network airing of the Toilet Tragedy episode on "Rescue 911" paid for the bulk of Bob's rehabilitation.

MORE GOOD REASONS NOT TO CLEAN

These case histories graphically point up the dirty truth that many things do not need to be cleaned at all and in fact fare far better than their cleaned counterparts. For example:

• *The outsides of popcorn kettles should never be cleaned.* The accumulation of grease and carbon creates a protective barrier that regulates range-top temperatures, preventing those nasty black pieces of popcorn hull that affix themselves to your teeth and those inconvenient raging fires so often associated with high-heat cooking.

• *Do not remove the scum from the shower soap dish.* Soap scum has adhesive properties that allow the bar of soap to stay put. Without this helpful substance, you may well find yourself in the emergency room, having to say something stupid like, "I broke my toe with a bar of Irish Spring."

• *Don't bother cleaning mirrors.* We all know how important our self-image is; if we think we're beautiful, we are beautiful. Sometimes we need a little help in this regard. The smooth, even haze provided by normal household air pollutants affords cosmetic benefits heretofore available only to aging Hollywood stars. Removing that film would allow you to see every wrinkle, blotch, and blemish. Images reflected by film-covered glass have a dreamlike, ethereal quality—achieving much the same effect as the camera lens filters used to shoot has-beens in cosmetic infomercials. The same effect can be achieved by removing your contacts before looking in the mirror.

5
Tools and Supplies
Stuff People Use to Clean Their Homes and Why You Don't Need It

You may have heard a rumor that there is a vast array of supplies and tools available to make cleaning simple, fast, and easy. You will discover, however, that THIS IS A LIE. None of these aids is going to make the process of cleaning any simpler, faster, and easier than the time-honored method of closing the door to the offending area, grabbing the car keys, and zooming off to the mall.

In fact, many of these energy-saving tools and products create *more* work, as these items will *also* need to be cleaned, maintained, and stored. Think of the fun you could have with a broom closet if it weren't so full of brooms.

If, however, you insist on having cleaning paraphernalia at the ready for moments when you are seized by uncontrollable nesting behavior caused by a microchip buried in your skull, the following guide will help you select the proper equipment.

VACUUM CLEANERS

The conventional wisdom is to purchase the very best you can afford. Of course, this wisdom is proffered by sales persons of obscenely overpriced vacuum cleaners, who, if they were capable of wisdom, would not be making their living by dumping powdered sugar and sand on your carpet.

Actually, you need not purchase a vacuum cleaner at all. Merely say "yes" to any offer of a free, no-obligation home demonstration. These offers come about once a week—a reasonable interval in which to accumulate in your carpet sufficient dirt, dog hair, twigs, and Grape-Nuts to justify having that obnoxious person in your house for two hours.

You will need to learn a few techniques in order to get rid of this person once he's finished the demonstration and begins strong-arm closing tactics:

• At a prearranged time, have a neighbor ring your phone. Reluctantly answer, then become distraught. Beg and plead to the "caller" that if he repossesses your car, you'll be unable to drive down and collect your unemployment check.

• An alternate script for the above prearranged call: Whisper quietly into the phone that, yes, he's here now, and you'll try to stall him as long as you can, but you think he's getting suspicious, and you're not sure you have enough nerve to go through with it anyway.

• In the last room you have the salesman perform his "demonstration," have lying around stacks and stacks of true crime tabloids. Cut out the particularly gory accounts and tape them all over the wall. A large piece of rotting meat hidden under the bed heightens the effect.

• When he begins the hard sell, drag out the photo albums and begin chattering. Nonstop. Do not take a breath. A detailed account of the prolonged, difficult, and complicated labor and delivery of each of your children is good. If you have fewer than four kids, make up more. Then move along to anguished chronicles of the resulting female problems that are suspiciously like the ones experienced by Aunt Fiona, whose pregnancy was, in fact, a fibroid tumor weighing slightly more than a Thanksgiving turkey.

• When he nears the end of his spiel, let your eyes glaze over, and begin slowly rocking back and forth while you hum "The Battle Hymn of the Republic."

SHOP-VACS: This is the carp of vacuum cleaners and, as such, is actually pretty handy to have around. Most vacuum cleaners are designed for the homes of the Domestically Gifted, which makes them very temperamental about what they suck up and therefore useless. If you must bend down and pick up every little chicken bone or deceased family pet before vacuuming, what good is it? By then, you'll have thrown out your back and your doctor will order you to take it easy and stay away from strenuous activities such as vacuuming.

In the sucking up department, however, Shop-Vacs are to carpet what Eddie Haskell is to June Cleaver.

DUST CLOTHS

Millions of people pay actual money for rags. This is ridiculous. The definition of a rag is a piece of waste cloth. A good rule of thumb is never to *buy* waste matter. Just as you would not offer negotiable currency for the contents of your neighbor's sink drainer or the trash bin in the men's room at the state park, be wary of the rag racket.

Why pay for waste when you have plenty of your own? Closets and dresser drawers—particularly *your* closets and drawers—are filled with suitable items. Start with your husband's underwear drawer. Anything with at least one hole in it can be appropriated. (*Note:* Most men's underwear comes with one *intentional* opening. Do not include this in your count.)

Most anything can be transformed into a rag by cutting it up or ripping it apart. Old towels make good rags. However, for most people, this means the entire contents of the linen closet. The only *new* towels in existence are those belonging to newlyweds from families with names like Smythe-Witherspoon. So you'll have to keep back some of your old towels for actual toweling-type activities, unless you plan on remarrying into old money.

Anything flannel is good. Your husband's plaid shirt is perfect, and will lend a wholesome, woodsy, Eddie Bauer feel to the proceedings, particularly if coupled with a pine-scented cleaner. Be sure to remove the buttons, so as not to scratch the furniture, and to discourage your husband from wearing it after you've used it to wipe out the diaper pail.

Warning: Do not use your child's blanky. He will grow up to be neurotic and will blame you for any reckless episodes involving automatic weapons.

Under no circumstances should you ever purchase

prepackaged dust cloths impregnated with cleaning chemicals. The expense is a total waste, because by the time you get around to actually using one of these things, it will have dried out and become beef jerky.

SPONGES

Sponges are actually the skeletons of dead sea creatures and, along with all other corpses and carrion, do not belong in your kitchen sink. If you wish to have some as under-sink decor, there are, of course, brightly colored synthetic sponges recycled from leisure suits confiscated from dances sponsored by Parents Without Partners.

FEATHER DUSTERS

The only appropriate use for one of these things involves a French maid's costume, garter belt and net stockings, and a camcorder in the bedroom. See the latest issue of *Penthouse* for further details.

BROOMS

There are several different kinds of brooms—regular brooms, whisk brooms, electric brooms, witch brooms, clothes brooms, utility brooms, push brooms—all of which get stored in the broom closet.

Apparently, the broom has achieved better than family member status, so it has its own room. What kind of skewed society gives a wooden dowel with corn-husk bristles its own room when Grandma has to sleep on the Little Mermaid air mattress in the basement?

Many people make the mistake of thinking that sweeping is cleaning. Brooms don't actually eliminate dirt; they merely relocate it. The dirt still sits there, but now it's in a pile that people can see and therefore avoid.

DUSTPANS

After a while, the piles of dirt you sweep up will accumulate into large mounds that people can no longer step over. They will block the flow of traffic and create fire-exit hazards. So you will need a dustpan. These are little shovels that can be used to scoop stuff up so it may be relocated to a less conspicuous area, such as your neighbor's patio.

MOPS

If you're not sure if you have a mop, check your garage. Most homes have at least three broken self-wringing sponge mops leaning up against the wall there. Because they are so very fragile, and will generally break after the first use, they are sold with a five-year replacement guarantee. Of course, no one ever collects on this, because who's going to spend the afternoon figuring out how to package and ship a five-foot mop?

The only unbreakable kind are those huge wooden-handled Medusa-looking affairs that sailors are always being ordered to swab something with. These will work if your kitchen floor approximates the area of an aircraft carrier deck and you prefer having it wet for three days at a time.

You will want to have the breakable kind so as to provide a constant excuse for why you haven't washed your floors. However, mops can be avoided altogether by keeping two or three Great Danes around the house.

TOILET BRUSH

This is a long-handled bristle affair that generally comes in its own holder, often designed to camouflage its true nature by masquerading as a plastic sunflower or other highly realistic bathroom-type vegetation.

The long handle does allow you to scrub the interior of the bowl without getting your hands near the offending areas; however, you then have a dripping brush, which, when left undisturbed in its holder for the next three or four months until you next have occasion to clean, will look like a Chia Pet.

SPECIALTY CLEANING ITEMS

There are cleaning tools designed for tackling a kajillion specific, unbelievably petty chores that you have no intention of doing anyway, such as cleaning miniblinds and sanitizing the spray nozzle on your showerhead. You can avoid these tools by removing your name from the mailing lists of catalogs that feature nose-hair clippers and musical toilet seats that play "Ol' Man River" when the lid is raised.

USEFUL THINGS YOU CAN DO WITH CLEANING STUFF THAT DOESN'T INVOLVE CLEANING

You might find that your home is cluttered up with useless cleaning items—perhaps brought into your home by a well-meaning but warped neighbor, or dragged in by the Rottweiler—and now you don't know what to do with them. The following ideas can help.

S.O.S. SOAP PADS: These make great shoulder pads for the Lenten season, when you wish to be penitent yet fashionable.

TOILET BOWL BRUSH: Just snap the handle off, spray the bristles green, and you have a festive holiday candle wreath for last minute gift giving.

HANDI-WIPES: Elegant as a hospital gown for the petite patient.

WHISK BROOM: Attach, bristles up, to the toilet seat to discourage dawdling.

MINIBLIND CLEANER: Remove the lamb's-wool covering on the "fingers" and you have a great "Freddie Krueger" prosthesis for the kiddies.

VACUUM CLEANER ATTACHMENTS: Cut up lengths of the hose to make leg warmers for arthritic Cabbage Patch dolls.

RUBBER GLOVES: Fill them with green tinted water and freeze. Then peel away the glove and tuck the resulting hand in amongst the peas in the produce section of the supermarket and scream incoherently something about sexual harassment and the Jolly Green Giant.

VACUUM CLEANER BAGS: These make charming yet suitably plain hair snoods for enormous Amish women.

HOUSEHOLD CLEANING PRODUCTS

MIRACLE SUBSTANCES
TO MAKE YOUR LIFE MORE EXPENSIVE

There exists nothing on this planet for which there does not exist an equal and opposite solvent, usually with a dopey name like Miracle Whizzzz or Whamm-Y or ZZZZIP. (The letters w, y, and z apparently have powerful hygienic connotations.)

These products are rarely given intelligent-sounding names, since most consumers like to think of themselves as smarter than their cleaning products. Too, people are likely to mistake the nature of a really cerebral-sounding product. A dish soap called Mensa, for instance, had to be pulled off the shelves because too many people thought it was a feminine hygiene product.

All of these products are required by law to make your kitchen, bathroom, or bedroom smell like Something Else. For instance, to be considered truly clean, a kitchen must not smell like a place where food is cooked. It must smell like an emergency room or a Christmas tree nursery. Bathrooms, on the other hand, should give the impression that food preparation involving lemons or strawberries often occurs in the vicinity, or that the last person to use the toilet sat there with a newspaper and a piña colada.

IS YOUR CLEANING PRODUCT SAFE
OR MERELY EFFECTIVE?

There are two kinds of cleaning products: Toxic and Nontoxic.

TOXIC: You can tell which ones these are by the hostile nature of their labels and copious use of capital letters and exclamation points, e.g., DANGER!!! HARMFUL WHEN SWALLOWED!!!! DO NOT USE!!!! CONTACT WITH SKIN WILL CAUSE YOU TO SPONTANEOUSLY COMBUST!! WILL CAUSE MOST SURFACES TO DIS-INTEGRATE!!!!! ABORT! ABORT!!! LASSIE, WHAT IS IT, GIRL?

The label will further instruct you not to use the product indoors, which is the primary location of the items you wish to clean. If you choose to disregard the warnings, you will be prosecuted.

NONTOXIC: These products come in a bottle with a label that proudly proclaims that it will clean every-thing you own, and that the remainder can be used as a nutritious breakfast supplement, baby formula, or lawn mower lubricant. You are encouraged to replace all existing cleaning products with this nonpolluting, harmless substance, which is evidently pumped from the surface of a magical, benevolent planet located in a galaxy known only to the manufacturers. Unfortu-nately, due to the different composition of our atmo-sphere, these products do not work on Earth.

INFOMERCIAL PRODUCTS

UNBELIEVABLE, AMAZINGLY
INCREDIBLE BREAKTHROUGHS

Why settle for the several thousand products available on supermarket and discount store shelves when you now have cable TV at your disposal? For those sleepless nights when you just can't stop worrying about how you're going to remove that chewing tobacco stain from your daughter's wedding gown, hope is at hand.

Fortunately for you, you're just a credit card number away from a miracle product that can clean anything, anywhere, at any time—except, as you will discover, in your own home. It will cost you only slightly more than the purchase price of the item you wish to clean. Postage and handling can be handled in three easy payments, in amounts normally referred to as "endowments."

These cleaning products are sold by people undergoing treatment for amphetamine abuse. Their major job qualification is a voice with the soothing tones of the Indy 500. The show is filmed before a live studio audience composed of individuals who are paid to act as if they are witnessing a reenactment of the Resurrection.

THE VINEGAR AND AMMONIA CULT

According to the domestic zealots, vinegar has more miraculous properties than the water at Lourdes.

According to legend, Our Lady of Perpetual Housekeeping appeared in an apparition to a young peasant girl named Heloise and told her to spread the good news about vinegar. This apparition so frightened the young girl that her hair turned white, and she started a household hints column to spread the message.

There will be people who tell you that you can clean just about anything with either vinegar or ammonia and a little bit of elbow grease. (Unfortunately, half of America is frantically searching the supermarket shelves for a product called Elbow Grease, while the other half is feverishly at work trying to extract this stuff from their elbows with breast pumps.)

Vinegar does in fact do a reasonable job on many items around the house. (In fact, Windex is now getting serious competition from Hidden Valley and Wishbone.) It will also give you an irresistible urge to set out little bowls of garbanzo beans and to install a sneeze guard over the entire living room.

(True Believers even use vinegar as a final rinse after shampooing their hair. Presumably, one should use wine vinegar for special occasions.)

Vinegar is often praised as a wonderful no-streak glass cleaner. Of course, this is ridiculous, since no such product exists. Nonstreaked glass must be obtained directly from the glass manufacturer.

Ammonia is also touted as a superior cleaning product. This is patently ridiculous. Everyone knows that ammonia is the main ingredient in dirty diapers. *Consumer Reports* studies show consistently inferior results when polishing the picture window with marinated Pampers.

Ammonia also stinks. Whatever you've cleaned with ammonia probably didn't smell as bad when it was dirty as it does now that it's clean. Instead of people remarking on how clean your house smells, they'll screw up their noses and ask you if you just gave your Mom a home perm near the air vents.

6
Preventive Measures
Don't Do the Grime if You Haven't Got the Time

Someone—probably Vince Lombardi, Benjamin Franklin, or a highly placed, anonymous State Department source (because they are responsible for most of the quotes in this country)—said, "The best defense is a good offense."

This applies to cleaning as well. Defend yourself against dirt! Children and pets are the biggest cause of dirt. Much of the cleaning that takes place is a result of improper planning or the neglect of a few simple routine steps—such as birth control and spaying.

In fact, experts agree that the single most useful household appliance for keeping your home clean is a diaphragm.

If you're reading this too late, here are some other preventive measures you can take.

TOILETS: Toilets are receptacles for nasty, unclean substances, so it's rather silly to aspire to a high degree of cleanliness in the bowl itself. It's the exterior of the bowl that causes the aesthetics problem. It is almost always due to a male whose accuracy of aim approximates a drunken elephant bathing itself.

The same men who create long-range missiles that can pinpoint a target the size of a Raisinet have difficulty regulating a stream of water from two feet. Should we not expect greater accuracy from young boys who regularly master the ultimate level with their Nintendo joysticks?

Preventive measures can help. Start young. If you are toilet training your male child, sprinkle some Cheerios into the bowl as dandy targets for sinking. Not only will your child be potty trained quicker (since he'll think he's playing an arcade game), he'll be learning valuable skills in accuracy, which will save you many hours of cleaning down the road.

Bonus: You can teach your child to read at the same time if you use Alpha-Bits.

If you are dealing with an adult male with a large ego, you might try retraining with glazed donuts. This is exceptionally effective with police officers.

TUBS AND SHOWERS: A membership in the local health club or YMCA affords a wonderful alternative to time-consuming cleanup following home bathing. Encourage your family to perform their daily ablutions in places where there is a paid staff to handle such nonsense. If they balk, close off the heating vents in bathrooms during winter months. Eliminate such temptations as towels and shampoo.

REFRIGERATORS: Cleaning out the refrigerator becomes totally unnecessary if you never put anything dirty in it to begin with. Food pretty much just sits there minding its own business and staying out of trouble, so if you just keep the door closed and away from coal chutes and oil refineries, you should be OK.

UPHOLSTERY: The simplest way to eliminate upholstery cleaning is to eliminate upholstery. All-wood furniture will stay clean and look good forever because no one will want to use it. Who wants to stretch out and watch the ball game on a piano bench?

This is why most historic mansions are furnished with spindly, uncomfortable wood furniture instead of futons. Grubby tourists with melting Sno-Kones and sweaty tank tops will look elsewhere to park their big behinds.

If you must have upholstery, make sure to keep plastic on it to deter people from sitting down. This is particularly effective during the summer, except with people who enjoy the smell of burning Spam and the sensation of lounging in hot candle wax.

FLOOR COVERINGS: Most traditional floor coverings need to be vacuumed, swept, mopped, or waxed, which is why you should avoid them. Dirt floors are preferable and the choice of billions of people worldwide for their low maintenance—the nature of dirt floors is that they *be* dirty. While your neighbors follow the herd with a Euro-chic, Southwestern, or country motif, your home can be a showplace for Third World decor. ("It's all the rage in Calcutta.")

If, however, you feel compelled to cover your floors, at least use your head when choosing color. For rugs and carpeting in high-traffic living areas, select a shade of brown similar to the soil in your area. Call your local university's agriculture extension service for advice.

If you live in an area without soil, such as New York City, you'll want to match the current shade of chalk used by NYPD for body outlines in your neighborhood, preferably with a dizzying pattern of O-positive colored splotches.

Dining room area rugs should be the color of barbecue sauce, gravy, and red wine. If you have small children, look for something in the SpaghettiO family.

THINGS THAT SHOULD NOT BE
IN YOUR HOUSE AT ALL

We've already discussed that children and pets should not be in your home. If you must have them, they are best kept in other people's homes, preferably those already equipped with domestic servants.

However, there are other things to avoid—things that are "designed to make your life easier"—that are, in fact, Additional Things to Clean. Check your home for these time and energy wasters:

APPLIANCE COVERS: Many otherwise intelligent people attempt to outsmart kitchen grease and keep tomato sauce particles from getting on their countertop appliances by disguising them as barnyard animals. These disguises are generally quilted pigs, cows, ducks, or roosters that double as protective gear and home decor. Unfortunately, these tacky little hoods fool no one, least of all kitchen gunk. So unless your can opener or toaster is planning to attend the Mardi Gras, lose the dippy little costumes.

TOILET-SEAT COVERS: These make as much sense as fire hydrant cozies on the dog-walk promenade. The makers of toilet seats specifically *chose* porcelain and fiberglass for their product because, unlike fake fur and shag carpeting, they are nonabsorbent—a desirable characteristic for items that come into contact with human waste. Nevertheless, millions of hygienically impaired people feel that a toilet should resemble the interior of a pimp's Eldorado.

BROOM, VACUUM, OR TOILET-BRUSH COVERS: Some people, notably those who have fallen through the cracks of the mental health care system, choose to play dress-up with their cleaning tools instead of putting them away. The Hoover gets a full dress maid's uniform and sits in the front hall, and the toilet brush becomes a whimsical Dutch girl peering out from behind the throne, her suspiciously yellow yarn braids saturated with odor-causing bacteria. Very few people are fooled by these disguises.

DRESSER SCARVES: Why does a dresser need a scarf? Apparently there is some concern that our dresser tops are getting chilled. This is nonsense. Scarves should be kept in the drawers, not on them, unless you *want* your bureau to resemble a Ukrainian peasant woman.

WINDOW SHEERS: Their only apparent function is to darken a room just enough to make reading impossible and to kill your houseplants. They do not provide any of the expected window-covering benefits, such as privacy, insulation, or room darkening. They do, how-ever, have magnetic properties for dirt, smoke, and anything the color of weak chicken broth. Their only advantage is that you can't see the filthy windows.

FURNITURE THROWS: These are intended to improve the looks of a really ratty couch or chair by hiding it under something slightly less ratty. So if you use furniture throws to keep your nice, expensive tasteful couch clean, people will assume you're hiding something. They'll smile condescendingly and work into their conversation a casual mention of the free cheese giveaway down at the church next Tuesday.

LAMPSHADE COVERS: These are nothing more than oversized shower caps. However, if you *want* to dress up your lamps as rap singers, go ahead.

7
Cooking
The Womanly Art of Turning Dead Animals and Shrubbery into Food

TEST TO DETERMINE THE EXTENT OF YOUR COOKING DISABILITY

1. *Do you think of Chef Boyardee as a father figure?*

2. *Have you written to the people at Kraft to demand that they call their fluorescent pasta "Cheese and Macaroni"?*

3. *Are you awaiting boil-in-bag broth?*

4. *Do you think the main ingredient in a "scratch" cake is Cruex?*

5. *Do you consider the oven a handy place to stash dirty dishes when company comes?*

6. *Do you think Calphalon is a brain disorder?*

7. *Have you ever tried to use MSG as a feminine hygiene spray?*

8. *Is your contribution to a pitch-in supper usually the paper products?*

9. *When you yell, "Soup's on!" do the children scratch their heads and say, "What's soup?"*

10. *Do you think Corningware is a brand of farm apparel?*

If you answered yes to more than one of these, you may be clinically Impaired. Not that this is a problem, you understand. Unless you live in an area where your entree is dragged home hanging by its hooves on poles borne by bearers clad in loincloths, your lack of food preparation skills is not going to be a problem.

After all, these days, when people refer to *cooking,* what most of them really mean is *defrosting.*

NAMING THE DISH

FUN WITH EUPHEMISMS

Cooking, like anything else, is a matter of perception. If it sounds delicious, people think it *is* delicious, especially if it sounds delicious in a foreign language—even if, roughly translated, it means "this would gag a goat."

So you've got to have a catchy name for your recipe. The French know this, which is why they made up *escargot* as a code name to replace the less appetizing word *snail.* French restaurants quickly learned that pâté de fois gras significantly outsold Mashed Goose Bile Duct Spread, even though they're the same thing.

The key here is to use a lot of syllables, preferably ones that require an adenoidal condition to pronounce correctly. You must endeavor to say them in a tasty sounding manner while imparting a sense of superiority—a preemptive snobbery that will prevent people from saying, "What the hell is that?"

Americans are starting to get the hang of this. It is far more appetizing to envision a Porterhouse smothered in mushrooms than a cow rump suffocating in fungus. And would people eat fried pig fat if it weren't called pork rinds?

Some other examples of artful noms de food:

CODEWORD	TRANSLATION
Bagels	Pound cakes that did not rise
Tapioca	Unsuccessful gravy
Sweetbreads	Animals who signed the organ donor card
Hasenpfeffer	Poached bunnies
Hot dish	Creamettes and whatever that was in the Tupperware
Dumplings	Boiled wallpaper paste
Tofu	Cubed Nerf balls
Fruitcake	Fossilized reindeer droppings
Aspic	Canned ham snot

STUFF THAT'S ACTUALLY GOOD
BUT SOUNDS INEDIBLE
Mud pie • Dirty rice • Pot stickers • Angel hair •
Gummi worms • Hush puppies • Pigs-in-a-blanket •
Bear claws • Elephant ears • Black cows •
Ladyfingers • Fuzzy Navels

With a little creativity, you can turn an ordinary foodstuff into an exotic treat—particularly if your children are young or your family is particularly stupid. For example:

- Tell them the little packets of mustard are "astronaut pudding."

- Explain that the stuff in the bowl is not Cream of Wheat but is, in fact, pureed spaghetti.

- Point out that what they, peasants that they are, perceive to be tuna casserole is actually *pasta du mer.*

- Inform them that the stuff smeared on their Wonder bread is *not* peanut butter. That it's *pâté de Skippy.*

CALL IT CUISINE

WHAT'S FOOD GOT TO DO WITH IT?

Definitely start using the word *cuisine.* People are always much more impressed with cuisine than they are with food, mostly because *cuisine* sounds really sophisticated, and *food* sounds more like a primitive grunt. This is why you have never seen a movie with a prehistoric apeman growling, "Me want cuisine."

The word *cuisine* implies expensive ingredients, skillful preparation, and artful presentation—characteristics not found in *food.* When was the last time you heard about an emergency airlift of cuisine to a wartorn Third World nation? How many highway signs read, "Gas, Lodging, Cuisine—This Exit"?

CONTINENTAL CUISINE

PUBLIC RELATIONS
TECHNIQUES FOR YOUR FOOD

Better yet, refer to all your food as *continental* cuisine. This conveys an elite perception, despite the fact that it's a meaningless affectation since most countries *are* located on continents, with the exception of places like Haiti, which have no food anyway.

Upgrade hot dishes and casseroles by calling them ratatouille or gumbo. Or if it's really awful, cover it and call it a Covered Dish. They can't say you didn't warn them.

ETHNIC CUISINE

HIDING BEHIND THE FLAG

Ethnic Cuisine is anything you would not normally eat unless you were stranded in the wilderness after a plane crash. This includes the internal organs of animals who fling themselves under the wheels of your car during drives through West Virginia. Other possibilities: parasitic insects, vermin, and the household pets of people whose names have no vowels.

Ethnic Cuisine is not the sole province of meat eaters. Many unappetizing plant items can be used to create ethnic cuisine for your vegetarian friends. Underground fungi sniffed out by trained European pigs are called *truffles*, which leads people to believe they're about to dine on Godiva chocolates. American pigs have not quite got the hang of sniffing out fungi, preferring instead to sniff each other.

You can turn the mystique of Ethnic Cuisine to your advantage by claiming that your botched rendition of a standard, well-known recipe is, in fact, an Ethnic Delicacy and haughtily informing the skeptics that it is *supposed* to taste like that, for goodness' sake! Here are a few guidelines to use when determining how best to pass off your pitiful cooking as Ethnic Cuisine:

TEX-MEX: Merely pour mass quantities of jalapeño salsa over anything and give it a Mexican-sounding name such as "Waffles Rancheros," or "Froot Loops Fajitas." Serve with Doritos and tequila and say "arriba!" a lot.

SCANDINAVIAN: Instantly transform a tasteless, bland, and colorless meal into an international taste treat by giving it a Scandinavian name. This is especially helpful when you are out of salt, pepper, or any other seasoning and is accomplished with the copious use of the letters *j* and *k*, preferably together, along with double vowels. Sprinkle with umlauts. For example, Special K and boiled grits become Kjärgriitsbäaker."

SOUTHERN: All you really need for true Southern cooking is a deep fat fryer and a U-Haul full of lard.

The cooking process is technically known as "frying up a batch." (The *up* is critical here.) Select an item on the American Heart Association danger list, plunge it into the fryer, and give it a folksy-sounding name, such as "Down Home Saturated Fatback Puppies." Serve in a napkin-lined basket, saving the napkin for recycling day at McQuik's.

FRENCH: Turn a ho-hum American meal into French cuisine by immersing it in wine and igniting it. Serve with a huge phallic loaf of hard bread and a superior attitude.

CHINESE: All you need for an authentic Chinese meal is the ability to slice the entire contents of your refrigerator on the diagonal. Be careful to use only enough meat to flavor the dish; the presence of actual rations of meat is a dead giveaway you have no idea what you're doing. Add rice cooked in wallpaper paste. Because you eat this stuff with wooden sticks instead of forks, this is the cuisine of choice for domestically impaired homemakers who have no clean silverware.

JAPANESE: Similar to Chinese cuisine, except you will need to perform drum majorette routines with a Ginsu knife while hurling the food about the room.

ITALIAN: Merely refer to noodles as pasta, and it's instant Italian. The beauty of this cuisine is that anything cooked in tomato sauce, oregano, and garlic suddenly becomes Italian, including wontons, which become ravioli. Or you can just drench everything in olive oil and give your dish a name that ends in -*illi* or -*ini*, e.g., Leanini Cuisini.

BRITISH: Anything pasty and inedible may pass as British food if it is called Something-shire Pudding; for example, Worcestershire Tuna Pudding. Or, adopting that strange British humor, you may disguise your overcooked meat by covering it with dough and calling it a pie.

POLYNESIAN: Open a can of pineapple chunks and pour it over whatever you're serving. Call it "Aloha Something-or-Other," or add lots of *w*'s and *ki*'s to the original name; for example, "Aloha Spam," or "Wikiwi-kiii Beans 'n' Weenies."

GERMAN: Boil everything in sugar and vinegar for 11 hours and give it a very long, stupid-sounding name like "Wienershnottschnauzerbraten." Serve with lots of warm beer, and make rude noises.

RUSSIAN: If you have a head of cabbage and a bunch of beets, it's party time in Leningrad! Boil them together for several days, longer if you live in an apartment building with screaming babies. Set a can of tuna on the table as a centerpiece. Serves 4 families.

CALIFORNIA NOUVELLE: This is an excellent way to disguise the fact that you haven't been to the grocery store in months. Anything run through a paper shredder and served in small enough portions can qualify as California Nouvelle, except for meat, which is not allowed at all. Advanced cooks will want to do intricate cosmetic surgery on their veggies to make them look like flowers or animals or Michael Jackson. Arrange the food with tweezers to make a picture on the plate. Call out for a pizza half an hour later.

SOUL FOOD: The internal organs of nocturnal animals that have not quite gotten the hang of crossing the street in traffic. They are highly spiced so as to disguise their true nature, and are referred to as *coon* and *possum* in an effort to obscure the fact that they are, in fact, *ra*ccoon and *o*possum, which are, of course, inedible. Hide the meat underneath a pile of shrubbery, called *greens*, that has been cooked in bacon grease and hope no one notices what's underneath.

EAST INDIAN: Merely add mass quantities of curry to whatever is in the fridge, except for cows, which should not be served since they may be a deceased relative. The strong flavor of curry is used to disguise monkey brains, so imagine what it can do for an inferior meat loaf or a tuna noodle casserole.

8
Cooking Utensils
Why You Don't Need Them

Many of your so-called standard, necessary kitchen utensils are merely symbolic artifacts used in the ritualistic rite of passage known as the bridal shower. For that reason they may have sentimental value, but why go out and spend good money on things you will never use? Besides, in your hands, they are undoubtedly lethal.

Cooking utensils can be classified into three main categories:

1. Gadgets for the Julienning of Fingers

2. Gadgets Whose Handles Melt When Left Near the Stove

3. Gadgets Whose Parts Wedge into the Back of the Drawer, Jamming It and Making It Impossible to Open

SAY GOOD-BYE TO
KITCHEN UTENSILS FOREVER

Tedious and dangerous chopping, slicing, and dicing can be eliminated by avoiding any food that requires any such nonsense. Opt for ready-to-eat foods that are, by nature, bite-sized. Peas are perfect. So are pearl onions, cherry tomatoes, and Milk Duds.

If you are forced into needing a kitchen utensil, there are other tools you already have in your home or garage that can substitute for whatever kitchenly-type task you have in mind, or you can circumvent the task altogether. Here a few safe, easy alternatives to those one-use white elephants jamming up your kitchen drawers.

MELON BALLER: You don't need this. Some pitiable souls have an unnatural compulsion to shape their fruit into cute little balls, perhaps due to a lack of childhood toys. These are usually the same people who whittle their radishes into chrysanthemums. If you get off on watching your cantaloupe roll around your plate into the baked beans, save yourself a lot of work and simply pick the fruit from the vine when it is very, very young and still small enough to cavort around the plate.

VEGETABLE PEELER: It is not necessary to peel vegetables or fruits unless you are eating them in a sanitation-impaired, fly-infested country where rinds are the leading cause of death. The peelings are usually the most nutritious part anyway, according to the National Pesticide Lobbyist League. Aside from the danger to dental work posed by unpeeled squash and coconuts—and that perplexed look people get when they peel onion skins off their tongues—leaving the skins on is a great work saver. In the event of a peeling-related emergency in which you absolutely must get that stuff off, you can effectively use a pencil sharpener for small carrots. Larger fruits and veggies can be handled with a liberal coating of Nair.

CHEESE GRATER: Surprise! Cheese now comes already grated (presumably from cows with perforated udders) and available for purchase at most grocery stores whose phone systems don't involve a hand crank and a woman named Cora. But if you find yourself stuck with a lump of cheese, you can shred large quantities by scrubbing the cheese across a screen door you've laid over the bathtub. Smaller batches may be grated by unscrewing the mouthpiece on your phone and rubbing the cheese over the holes.

FLOUR SIFTER: Only people who bake from scratch need one of these things, which naturally leaves you out. If, inexplicably, you do find yourself in need of sifted flour, place a large bowl outside the screen door. Taking careful aim, hurl the flour through the screen. Do not do this on a windy day.

COLANDER: This large, unwieldy bowl with holes in it only serves to ensure that you can't close the cupboard door. If you need to drain spaghetti or something, a tennis racket works just as well. For large quantities of pasta, toss the whole pot at the screen door. (See "Flour Sifter.")

GRAVY SEPARATOR: This gadget, designed to separate the fat from the meat juices, makes tedious work of a simple project. You can accomplish the same thing faster and easier by standing in a clean roasting pan and pouring the drippings over you. Anything that adheres to your thighs is fat and is the stuff you want if you are cooking Southern.

MEAT TENDERIZER: This spiked mallet, which resembles a medieval weapon used by psychotic knights of yore, is used to beat particularly tough cuts of meat into submission. The process is, in fact, a form of *prechewing*, and is called "rumination" in dairy cattle and camel circles. This disgusting practice is not necessary unless you buy cheap meat. Or just lay the cheap meat on the floor and do aerobics while wearing golf shoes.

GARLIC PRESS: No need to have this gadget cluttering up your drawers—not when you can have a year's supply of fresh garlic with one easy effort. Simply stuff your bra with garlic cloves on the day of your annual mammogram, and when the technician looks the other way, arrange the cloves around your breast between the X-ray plates. After she smashes the plates together, she will sniff the air and give you a Look; smile sweetly and say you had lunch at the Olive Garden.

PASTRY BRUSH: The only time you'd need a pastry brush is if you were going to make pastry, which is never, or for painting your turkey with butter so people don't break a tooth on the skin. So for those rare times when you'd actually use a pastry brush, use a large blusher brush, or just soak a sponge in butter and wring it out over the bird.

SMALL KITCHEN CONVENIENCE APPLIANCES AND WHY THEY'RE NOT CONVENIENT

The first rule is to never buy anything advertised as a "revolutionary food preparation" item sold on TV infomercials that pretend to be cooking shows with audiences that gasp and applaud as if they had just witnessed Yasir Arafat kissing Yitzhak Shamir. They behave in this manner because, by and large, they are stupid, but mostly because they are being paid to do so after having been trucked in from the unemployment line.

The second rule is never buy a small kitchen "convenience" appliance advertised as this year's hottest new gift. It will be relegated immediately to the basement after one use, along with the year's hottest new gift from each preceding year since the discovery of electricity.

Do not buy the following gadgets under any circumstances.

FOOD PROCESSOR: In a time of great outcry against so much processed food, who's the brilliant marketing expert that named this puppy? These expensive mini-workshops are touted as incredible work- and time-savers, eliminating countless hours of tiresome chopping (once you've finished hand-chopping the food in order to fit it into that little opening). You'll *need* all that saved time to clean out all the little parts with a toothpick. Scrap the monstrous doohickey and have your kid put the cole slaw through his Play-Doh Fun Factory.

SANDWICH MAKER: Since making a sandwich is apparently such a major culinary undertaking, the great scientific minds of the world dropped their atomic research in order to make life just a little easier for the American housewife, the result of which is an electric sandwich maker. The apparent drawing card on this is its ability to magically transform two slices of white bread *filled with* stuff into two slices of white bread *sealed around* stuff.

FOOD DEHYDRATOR: If you are planning to become paranoid and head for the hills to wait out nuclear war, this might come in handy for ration preparation. But you certainly don't need an expensive apparatus that sucks the moisture out of food and turns everything into Doggy Rawhide Chews when you can do that by simply leaving the food on a plate in the back of the fridge.

WAFFLE IRONS: These contraptions make gigantic messes out of perfectly good pancakes, your countertop, and the appliance itself, all of which you could do by yourself. If you feel the need to have flapjacks with geometric designs, merely stomp on them while wearing L. L. Bean hiking boots or lay them on the driveway and back up the Jeep.

JUICERS: This is simply an overpriced blender with a NASCAR engine used to make liquids out of things that nature went through a great deal of trouble to create as solids. If you chew properly, your digestive system will do this on its own for free.

BREAD MAKERS: Why make bread in an oven when you can spend hundreds of dollars for an appliance that makes nothing *but* bread and will pay for itself after only 7,465 uses? Of course, you have no intention of making bread anyway, so this whole conversation is ridiculous.

WHAT TO DO WITH THOSE KITCHEN GADGETS ALREADY IN YOUR HOME THROUGH NO FAULT OF YOUR OWN

You may already have dozens of unneeded kitchen utensils, due to the ignorant manner in which your friends and relatives select gifts. These need not go to waste if you exercise a bit of creativity and find uses for these things that more accurately reflect *your* interests, which have nothing to do with cooking.

ANGEL FOOD CAKE CUTTER: Most people who have one of these things don't even realize what it is and just assume it was something the builders left in the drawer when the house was originally built. However, if you happen to be a country western singer or televangelist, it is a great groomer for Big Hair.

TURKEY BASTER: This is useful as a nasal aspirator for large animals with sinus problems. Or you can leave it sticking out of your briefcase if you wish to deter strangers from striking up conversations with you on the airplane.

BLENDERS: You will want to keep this around for making delicious breakfast drinks such as margaritas and daiquiris. Also keep one handy by the phone with some ice cubes in it for those times when long-winded, boring people call. ("OOPS! Gotta go! The kids just threw the Waterford vase down the disposal.")

FUNNELS: Little funnels are perfect little prosthesis feet for those Barbie dolls your kids have mutilated. Her little legs stick neatly in the small end, and the large end helps balance her, which is good, considering how top-heavy she is. Larger funnels are effective child disciplinary devices: tell the offending child that if the behavior continues, you will wear it on your head next time you pick him up at school.

ROLLING PIN: This does serve an actual cooking purpose in a domestically impaired household as a gravy de-lumper. Spread your gravy out on a cutting board and roll until smooth. Later, use it to roll out those kinks and knots in sore leg muscles after a long day of shopping. Also works wonderfully for smoothing lotion on your huge mother-in-law's back.

GARLIC PRESS: With a hunk of Play-Doh and a garlic press, you can squeeze out great-looking miniature dolly hair. Or you can put green Play-Doh through the press to make little parasitic-looking things for a good-natured prank on your doctor during your next ear exam. Oh, how he'll laugh!

WIRE WHISK: These things are great as birthday gifts for children who have catered parties with ponies and clowns and professional photographers. Merely gift wrap a wire whisk with a gallon jug of bubble soap and present it as an Avant-Garde Bubble Blower you purchased during your last trip to the Louvre gift shop.

NUTCRACKER: Tell your daughter it's a Thighmaster for her Barbie doll.

9
Culinary Sleight of Hand
Tricking the Troops

PASSING OFF PREPARED, STORE-BOUGHT FOOD AS HOMEMADE

Most people screw up by trying to pass off a professionally prepared, perfect food item as their own made-from-scratch masterpiece. No one will believe *you* made it if it's flawless, so the addition of flaws is crucial here. Too, you must always remember to remove the original wrapping or serving container, making sure you hide it in the trash underneath something no one will touch, such as a used diaper.

CAKE: Mess up the perfect frosting swirls with the back of something. A shovel will do. Sprinkle the whole thing with powdered sugar and shove M&Ms into the sides. Dab your nose with frosting.

PIES: Drop onto a clean floor—which you can locate in any decorator showcase—then scrape up with a putty knife into your own baking dish. Dust some flour on the counter and paste some wet apple peelings to the side of the sink. (This is especially convincing if it's an apple pie.)

COOKIES: Refrigerated cookie dough works fine, but it's the uniform shape of the finished cookies that gives them away. Be sure to moosh the perfect circles with the heel of your hand a little before baking, and press a couple together to make some odd sizes. Or buy cookies from the bakery and put them in the toaster until they burn. Fill a large mixing bowl with hot sudsy water to leave in the sink.

BREAD: Buy unsliced loaves of bread and put them into loaf pans in the oven. Just as your family arrives home, turn up the furnace thermostat to 90°F, then zap a cup of beer in the microwave for that seductive aroma of warm yeast.

JAM: Spoon a bunch of Smucker's Strawberry Jam into tiny little jars with the red tops you've saved from bouillon cubes. Tie gingham checked ribbons around them and slap on terminally cute labels saying, "From My Kitchen to Yours," which is pretty much the truth, unless you did it in the bathroom.

MASHED POTATOES: Instant mashed potato flakes, many of whom are fondly called "Bud," can be passed off as real if you just microwave a large potato until it's thoroughly cooked, then scoop out the potato into the instant stuff, thereby providing the necessary lumps to convince anyone you made them from scratch. Peel one potato and slap the peelings on the side of the sink and on the fridge.

GRAVY: The smooth texture and meat flavor of canned gravy is problematic when you're trying to pass it off as homemade. However, if you add several cups of bacon grease and some hunks of moistened flour, it just may be bad enough to slide by.

THE OTHER SIDE OF THE COIN

PASSING YOUR HOMEMADE
FOOD OFF AS STORE-BOUGHT

Because of your undoubtedly well-deserved reputation in the kitchen, your family may be slightly more enthusiastic about take-out food. This, however, can get very expensive, and you may occasionally have to resort to actual home cooking. Of course, the downside is no one will want to eat it.

So how do you get your family to react to your cooking with the same euphoria they exhibit toward fast food?

Simple! First, save up those white paper bags, styrofoam boxes, and cardboard cartons. Then wrap whatever it is you've made in tissue paper that you've soaked in Mazola and shove it into one of those boxes/bags/cartons. Put on your coat, leave the house for a while, come in the back door looking harried and exhausted, and throw the stuff on the table. Be sure to put out a stack of fast food–type napkins, which you can obtain from any gas station's restroom toilet paper dispenser.

FOODS THAT HAVE NEVER BEEN
SUCCESSFULLY DUPLICATED AT HOME

ICE CREAM: There is no such thing as *good* home-made ice cream. It is a myth. If it were possible to produce good homemade ice cream in one's home, Ben & Jerry would be standing on an exit ramp with a sign saying "Will work for food."

CHEESE: Making this stuff is a disgusting process involving unappetizing-sounding words like *curds*, which is probably why the government is always trying to give it away.

PICKLES: Pickles made at home bear no resemblance whatsoever to the crisp deli ones you have come to expect. That's because all the recipes for homemade pickles were written by the people at Claussen and Vlasic, who *want* your pickles to turn out like flaccid frankfurters so you will keep buying theirs.

BREAD: The country is full of bakeries staffed by people who *know what they're doing*. They are professionals, whereas you are an amateur. Besides, the advantage of home-baked bread is not the *bread*, but the tantalizing aroma filling the house, which you can easily duplicate by stuffing store-bought pumpernickel into hot air vents. Keep in mind that if you *do* bake bread, the only thing likely to fill your house will be the screech of the smoke alarm.

10
The Language of Cooking
Nothin' Says Lovin' Like
Somethin' Stuck to the Oven

HOW TO INTERPRET RECIPES

SPOTTING THE ONES
THAT WANT TO POISON YOU

Many of the recipes that run in magazines look suspiciously like they were written by disgruntled postal employees on the last day of their employment. Therefore, you must exercise discernment in order to determine which ones are Real Recipes and which ones are Revenge Recipes that will, if you make them, mark you as an idiot for life.

If it is a Revenge Recipe, your family will rename the recipe to more aptly describe the concoction and bring it up at every opportunity: "Remember the time Mom made us eat Peach Glue and we got our stomachs pumped?"

First, beware of recipe names containing the word

71

surprise. Birthday surprises are nice. Breakfast surprises are not. Food should not be *sprung* on people like a paper snake in a peanut-brittle jar. Ask yourself, just what is it about this recipe that is so surprising? The unexpected gastrointestinal reaction?

Next, watch out for the word *medley.* While perfectly appropriate in musical compositions or as the baritone half of the Righteous Brothers, in cooking, *medley* is a red flag that the recipe will require you to mix foods that have no business being in the same kitchen together, much less on the same plate. If the foods belonged together, they'd come right out and say it, like Chicken Noodle Soup. So you'll see recipes coyly referred to as Ocean Garden Medley, because they can't just blurt out Squid Pumpkin Butterscotch Casserole.

Avoid recipes calling themselves Creamed Something-or-Others. Think back on creamed things you've eaten in the past—creamed corn, creamed beef on toast. Do you see a pattern here? Is this something you wish to perpetuate?

Beware of recipes that require spices that the neighbor you borrow from doesn't have. If it were a spice that you would want to put in your food, she'd probably already have it. Be especially wary of spices you've never heard of. There may be very good reason why you've never seen them as ingredients in any other recipe.

Finally, scan the preparation instructions for complicated procedures that require you to add the ingredients in a particular order, as if the butter *cares* whether it goes in before or after the eggs. Like they would *know?*

Avoid recipes whose instructions contain unreasonable demands on your time, such as "stir constantly," or "baste occasionally."

Most suspect are recipes that claim to duplicate an actual Good Recipe but with only half the fat and half the calories. This only works if you are dumber than a box of rocks and are easily fooled by cheap imitations. If you throw your panties on the stage when an overweight bus driver puts on a white jumpsuit and lip-synchs "Hunka hunka burnin' love," you just might be fooled into thinking carob tastes like chocolate.

BASIC LINGO

THE BUZZWORDS OF THE
COOKING BIZ FOR THOSE IN THE KNOW

EGGS: When a recipe calls for an egg, it means a chicken egg. You can't use just any egg. Many recipes have been ruined by the use of alternative eggs, such as those produced by ostriches, lice, and panty-hose companies.

MILK: Always be sure to use the kind that comes from cartons or bottles. Mother's milk, coconut milk, and milk of magnesia do not achieve the same culinary results.

SALT: Any recipe calling for salt probably means the kind that comes in those teensy little packets at the drive-thru. The stuff in your water softener gives inferior results.

OIL: In the context of a recipe, oil usually means vegetable oil with a name like Mazola or Wesson. Avoid brands like Pennzoil or Quaker State. Virgin olive oil is supposed to be good, but many people find it uncomfortable to delve into the sexual histories of their groceries.

PORTIONS: Ignore any references to how many people this recipe is supposed to serve unless everyone in your family has their jaws wired shut. When a recipe says "serves four," it doesn't say four *what.* An educated guess would be "four gerbils."

MEASUREMENTS: TBL (pronounced "tibble") means tablespoon, and TSP (pronounced "tisp") means teaspoon. They are not interchangeable modes of measurement; the difference between one tisp and one tibble of Tabasco sauce can mean the difference between a tasty meal and bleeding ulcers.

A cup (pronounced "cup") should be measured with a measuring cup, and not with your giant-sized commuter coffee mug or Aunt Anita's bra.

OZ (pronounced "ozz") means ounce, and should be avoided, because the only way to measure ounces is on a postage scale, which means waiting in line for three hours at the post office for a surly clerk who will eat whatever it is you're weighing.

SAUTE: This is the word people on fat-restricted diets must use when frying foods in order to avoid snippy lectures from their doctors and skinny relatives. It operates under the same premise as calling a tax an "investment contribution," only sautéeing actually produces a usable product.

BRAISE: Since boiled meat sounds so unappetizing, home economists suggest the use of the word *braise* to describe meat prepared in the same manner used by settlers to dye wool.

BROIL: Any food cooked by direct exposure to heat is considered broiled. Consequently, you can salvage that stuff that falls onto the heating element of the stove when the pot boils over by scraping it up and serving it as Broiled Foam.

KNEAD: This word means pushing, squeezing, stretching, pressing, pounding, and pummeling your food. It is the culinary equivalent of doing your laundry by hand at the side of the river, and is far too much work. You might want to simply send it out to a massage parlor and pick it up later.

DREDGE: Instead of coming right out and saying "cover with flour," recipes tell you to dredge your food. No one knows why recipe writers do this, but then, no one knows why bridge players have to give their bids in code. Why not just come out and say, "I have four hearts, none of them worth squat"?

BEAT: Beating is a vigorous, angry sort of stirring, and should go on and on and on until your arm falls off. You can also use an electric beater, which is not only easier on the arm, but provides wonderful spin-painting artwork for the kitchen walls, such as you would find at carnival midways. If you're going to let the kids lick the beaters, make sure you turn off the mixer first.

CULINARY ETIQUETTE

HOW TO KEEP YOUR WORDS FROM GETTING YOU SMACKED IN THE MOUTH

Though you may not do much cooking, there will be times when you will encounter people who do. It is important to be sensitive to their feelings, since growing up Different is difficult in a society that values conformity. When you encounter one of these persons, try not to stare at her apron, and avert your eyes if she has to mince or dice anything. It is important that you try to make her feel as comfortable as possible.

You may not have ever encountered homemade food before, but try not to act shocked. It may look and smell strange to you, but to her, this is the custom of her people.

Here are a few tips on what to say:

GOOD: "What's that delicious aroma wafting through the kitchen?"

BAD: "What's that smell coming from the kitchen?"

WORSE: "What's that odor stinking up the kitchen?"

GOOD: "You do have *such* a flair for the unusual!"

BAD: "Nobody else cooks that way."

WORSE: "Were you drunk when you made this?"

GOOD: "My, what an unusual flavor."

BAD: "My, this tastes strange."

WORSE: "My gawd! People EAT this &%$#??"

11
Laundry
A Frank Discussion of a Filthy Subject for Mature Adults

Unlike many dirty topics, this particular dirty topic is not at all titillating, and the only rush you're going to get out of it is the mad dash you make to catch the rinse cycle so you can add the fabric softener.

LAUNDRY: ITS ORIGINS AND REPRODUCTIVE METHODS

One of the unpleasant side effects of wearing clothes is that it creates laundry.

Clothes in the store or in your closet are *clothing*, once they are worn, however, they become *laundry*. They undergo a transformation similar to that of the straw spun by Rapunzel, only without the capital gains.

This transformation is caused by a complicated chemical process involving equations and unintelligible words such as *integer* and *cofactor*. Consequently,

77

doing laundry requires you to use things with chemicals in them, like water, which contains something called H_2O.

Laundry has developed a hardy reproductive system to ensure the survival of its species. Like its prolific ancestral counterparts (the cockroach, the zucchini, and the Osmond family), laundry breeds and reproduces practically overnight. It is thought to be one of the few textiles that take seriously the biblical injunction to "be fruitful and multiply."

At first, scientists theorized that laundry was capable of asexual reproduction, like earthworms, who play with themselves. However, with the aid of the electron microscope, researchers discovered that it is actually a two-garment affair, with fertilization commonly occurring during the union of buttons and buttonholes. Alternative lifestyles, while not completely accepted by mainstream laundry, include sleeves, zippers, pockets, and, in rare cases, the loops on the backs of oxford shirts.

Laundry not equipped with the normal sexual organs has evolved and adapted so that it may reproduce at will through artificial insemination. Socks are the most frequent donors and are fairly promiscuous. They rarely stay with their mates for long, preferring instead to go off and impregnate young impressionable dish towels.

Such reproductive habits make it imperative that the homemaker properly monitor her laundry's free time. Left alone with the door shut, it will inevitably do what laundry does and let nature take its course. While scientists are working on a safe, effective contraceptive for laundry, at this time there is no

100 percent effective method available to you. If you wish your laundry to refrain from "doing the dirty," there are some marginally useful products that can slow down its fertility rate: Tide with Spermicide (*Consumer Reports* rank **+) and Estrogen-Free Purex (**−).

ALTERNATIVES TO LAUNDRY

THERE MAY BE ANOTHER WAY

There are several approaches you can take to avoid or minimize laundry.

1. Get rid of all your washables and replace them with things made from fabrics that cannot be laundered, such as rhinestone. (Many of your country western singers got their starts just this way; they hated country music, but hated laundry even more.) Wood and masonry products are also good options, although none of these are particularly suitable for bed linens, bath towels, or diapers.

2. Become a nudist. It's important that the whole family go along with this. Otherwise, you'll still have to do *their* laundry. Of course, when they put you in that nice home with the friendly orderlies, someone else will do *your* laundry.

3. Become filthy rich. This is the simplest (and most appealing) of your options. Once you're filthy rich, like Cher, you can wear things like playpen mesh and dog harnesses (which require little laundering and no pressing) and call them clothing.

Or, if you're rich but engaged in a line of work

that, unlike MTV videos, requires actual clothing, you can simply buy new clothes anytime you want to get dressed, or you can hire lots of fastidious-type people to tend to the hygiene of your massive, fabulous wardrobe.

THE HOWARD HUGHES
SCHOOL OF LAUNDRY

If you're really wallowing in the dough, you can just forego laundry altogether since being filthy rich allows you to engage in all sorts of eccentric behavior, such as being filthy. People will like you for who you are—a very, very rich person.

For example, you can wear the same grody outfit for 11 years, and people will admire your refreshing lack of pretense. They will begin to feel self-conscious about their own tidy appearance. Fearing that their own clean shirts and pressed trousers betray an unsophisticated, working-class mentality, they will begin showing up with appropriately rank underarm perspiration rings that reek of old money.

Of course, in order to become filthy rich, you will have to acquire money in large amounts—which makes this an impractical option for people who have not had the opportunity to attend a Tom Vu seminar or talk to a counselor on the Psychic Friends Network. So you will probably have to, at some point in your life, Do Laundry.

12
How to Do Laundry
Getting Your Clothes Clean Without Ruining Them

TIPS ON SORTING

One of the first things you need to learn about washing is how to sort your laundry. This is called Making Piles.

You will want a separate pile for everything (remember those reproductive habits), so choose a large, clean work area, such as you might find in someone else's home.

First, separate all clothes collected from your children's bedroom floor or clothes hamper. These are clean, and need only to be refolded and put away. The dirty ones are (a) being worn, (b) in a school locker or gym bag, or (c) composting in the backyard.

Next, separate soiled clothes according to degree of disgust. The presence of flies, decomposition, or fossilized matter will help guide you. Then, further separate clothes into the following piles:

81

Darks*   Whites
Colors*   Mulattos

*You can distinguish between darks and colors with a simple test. Pour motor oil on the fabric. If the stain can be seen from a distance of two feet, it's a color.

While civilized countries throughout the world condemn and reject the practice of discrimination, it is still an acceptable practice in the laundry room. At this writing, the civil right of dark socks to freely associate with white underwear has not been recognized.

Note: When separating according to color, it is important to use the *original* color of the garment as your guide, not its current, soiled color.

Now the piles must be subdivided according to fabric. Make separate piles for the following, making sure you keep the previous separations intact:

Cottons   Silks
Colorfast cottons   Permanent press
Pre-shrunk cottons   Wools
Cotton blends   Delicates
Synthetics   Polyester double knits*

*Cover this pile so no one sees it.

You should now have 57 piles. Now look at the label inside each garment for washing instructions. Each one will say "wash separately." This is self-explanatory. Put those in separate piles.

You should now have 1,472 piles, none of which you *can* wash, because most washing machine manufacturers advise only running full loads. The only thing you can wash separately while fulfilling your full-load obligation is a bedspread—unless you are doing laundry for an enormous person whose under-pants come with a matching dust ruffle and pillow shams.

WHICH TEMPERATURE TO USE?

People who know about such things offer the helpful rule of thumb to use the hottest temperature that is safe for the fabric. This is very helpful advice if you happen to know the flash point of corduroy but overall is about as useful as a recipe that says, "Cook until done."

Ignore the hot water advice. There are some stains that, if washed in hot water, will actually meld with the fabric in a sort of cosmic textile oneness. Egg yolk and blood are famous for this—something to keep in mind if you find yourself at a particularly violent breakfast buffet.

(Also, should you be murdered, you can help inves-tigators convict the perpetrator by having the presence of mind to splatter some of your blood on his clothing and then throwing hot water on him.)

If you're on a low-cholesterol diet so that egg stains aren't much of a problem, and you don't bleed much, warm water should cover just about anything. Just set the dial on WARM and then break off the control so no one can boil your sweaters by accident.

If you still insist on selecting a temperature, the

key is to be able to differentiate between HOT, WARM, and COLD. This is somewhat like the labeling on salsa. It is only after purchasing a jar of MILD salsa and consuming your first bite that you learn that the taster who assigns the designations of MILD, HOT, and EX-TRA HOT is a gentleman named Juan Paco Pepe Garcia Jalapeño Martinez Tabasco. *You* will think you are using warm water; your hand-knit cardigan from Scotland will say "HOT!" and transform itself into a potholder.

WHAT ABOUT DETERGENT?

FUN WITH PHOSPHATES

It is interesting to note that we use detergent on items we intend to put on our feet, like socks, and merely *rinse* items that we intend to put in our mouths, like lettuce.

This is backward. Lettuce is grown in the dirt, marinated in toxic pesticides, and then handled by several hundred strangers, many of whom have nicknames like Ratboy and Turd.

According to the Centers for Disease Control, there have been no documented cases of tube sock poisoning in the United States. (When was the last time you heard someone say, "I'm not feeling so good. Must be something I wore on my feet."?) Very little of what loiters on athletic hosiery finds its way into our gastrointestinal tract or bloodstream, yet these are the things we soak and scrub and pretreat and bleach.

So, from a health standpoint, you should be using

detergent on your salad, not your laundry. Cheer with Blue Cheese is a good choice.

If, however, you still feel compelled to wash your clothes with detergent, keep in mind the following information when selecting a brand.

QUALITIES TO LOOK FOR IN A DETERGENT

• *Gets your clothes whiter than white.* This is helpful if you're a nurse in Anchorage who is frequently overlooked for promotions—simply because they can't see you. This detergent will provide the contrast you need to get ahead.

• *Will wash in all temperatures.* This feature is desirable in a detergent, since most climates vary from day to day, and you'll want to be sure your detergent is equally effective when it is sunny, partly cloudy, frigid, etc. The choice of meteorologists.

• *Safely bleaches colors.* If you've had the unfortunate experience of being run over, breaking an arm, or putting out your eye while bleaching colors in the past, you'll be pleased to know that there are now detergents that make this a much safer activity. Recommended by Ralph Nader.

• *Soaks clothes clean in cold water.* An excellent detergent for people living in areas of cold climates not served by utility companies whose terrain is characterized by large amounts of standing water.

• *Softens clothes while you wash*. This is detergent with fabric softener. In years past, homemakers wasted, on average, 127 hours per year waiting for the second rinse to add the fabric softener. They believed that if they put it all in together, something unspeakable would happen, such as the sorts of things experienced by people who rip off mattress tags. One day, a househusband in Fresno—a reckless bon vivant with a death wish—donned his Masters of the Universe helmet, threw caution to the wind, and put it *all in the washer together*. Thanks to that brave man, we now have all-in-one detergents.

• *Clothes come out sparkling*. The active ingredient in such detergents is glitter. While they are the official detergents of the Ice Capades, they are not a particular favorite of Mennonites.

STAIN REMOVAL—OUT, DAMNED SPOT!

You must learn to distinguish between Regular Uncleanliness and Stains. Regular Uncleanliness is pretty easygoing and cooperative, like an old wino who leaves the first time you ask. Stains, however, are more like Moonies and require you to engage in strange, ritualistic behavior to get rid of them. You must get in their face and literally *shout* at them. Products are made to do that for you, saving you the embarrassment of yelling at your underwear.

Brutally bombard these spots before laundering or they will become what is known as "set-in stains," a very serious condition resembling Mikhail Gorbachev's forehead.

The thing to remember about stains is that you will never remember what *removes* a stain and what *sets it in.* Here's a handy guide to consult at the spur of the moment, when stains first strike.

• *Red wine stains* can be removed with white wine. Well, actually, it just makes it a pink wine stain, which is less noticeable than a red stain.

• *Port wine stains* can be removed by a dermatologist.

• *Ballpoint ink* can be removed with hairspray. This was discovered back in the fifties, when fans on "American Bandstand" noticed that Annette Funicello and Frankie Avalon's signatures were mysteriously disappearing from autograph books.

• *Blood stains* respond to cold water and salt or meat tenderizer. According to forensics experts, however, all traces of blood are never entirely eradicated. Therefore, if the bloodstain in question would cause you any personal unease in a court of law, it is suggested that you soak the item in salty cold water such as the Dead Sea.

• *Grass stains* will not come out of good clothes. However, they will come out of old unattractive clothes with a paste made from powdered detergent, baking soda, and water. Liberally apply paste to stain. After a few hours, wash garment in hot water. The stain will come out, but because you used hot water, your favorite dress will now fit Malibu Barbie.

• ***Rust stains*** can be removed by rubbing with hydrogen peroxide and hanging out in the sun. This is exactly what preteen girls do when they want to look like Rod Stewart.

REMOVING STAINS
FROM YOUR CHILDREN

While not considered laundry per se, children often exhibit an affinity for Close Encounters of the Indelible Kind.

You might as well accept that your kids will, at some point, get into something that will not come off. This will invariably happen just prior to your scheduled family portrait sitting or other important event.

The nature of the Indelible substance will always be whatever is the most highly inappropriate for the circumstances. For example, if your son is about to have an audition to be the poster child for the Rough and Tumble All-Boy Mini-Macho line of blue jeans, he will get into your make-up drawer and cover himself in Revlon Coral Sunset lipstick, designed to maintain its fresh color throughout the entire Iowa growing season.

If your darling daughter is scheduled to meet with the nuns of Our Lady of Perpetual Tuition Preschool to consider her admission application, she will let the neighborhood teens draw obscene tattoos on her face with laundry marker.

Unfortunately, there are no effective ways to remove such stains that do not also require subsequent visits to the dermatologist.

ALTERNATIVES TO TIME-CONSUMING CONVENTIONAL METHODS OF LAUNDRY

GETTING AROUND IT

1. Put your laundry into the oven on SELF CLEAN. (This is an excellent tip, as it combines tasks, which is one of the Seven Effective Habits of Highly Annoying People.)

2. Check the weather report daily. When rain is forecast, put all your laundry out in the driveway and squirt some liquid detergent on it. If they're intermittent showers, you can even run out and add fabric softener to the last rinse.

3. Bundle up all your dirty laundry. Go to the laundromat. Wait until a Domestically Gifted–looking grandmotherly type arrives. Start stuffing everything into the washer—jeans and tennis shoes and lace tablecloths and diapers and oily rags—and then ask her if she thinks you should add the starch *with* the fabric softener and bleach or if it goes in *after* the Lime-A-Way. Then sit back while she takes over.

4. When taking a trip to visit your mother, pack all your dirty clothes into your suitcase. When she picks you up at the airport, inform her of the outrageous incident where the baggage handlers dumped open your suitcase on the runway.

5. Much laundry can be postponed by employing the fashion technique of *layering*, in which you put clean stuff over the dirty stuff. Cover a dirty blouse with a clean sweater. When the sweater's dirty, put on

a blazer. When the blazer gets sticky, add an overcoat. In an emergency, a school crossing-guard poncho fits nicely over the overcoat. Your coworkers may think the butter has slipped off your noodles, especially if you live in Tucson, but at least they won't think you're a slob.

13
Household Hints
Why You Should Ignore Them

There were roughly 925,456 household hints published in newspapers and women's magazines last year. Fourteen of them had some perceivable value. The remaining 925,442 are altogether useless, and are consequently listed in the Congressional Record. In fact, they form the basis for operations manuals at most government facilities.

Unfortunately, they also turn up in your magazines and newspapers next to Real News written by Actual Journalists containing quotes from the Queen of England. This is not an accident. Editors know that the casual reader is far too casual to notice things like column separations and will therefore immediately conclude that the Royal Family removes chewing gum from their hair with ice cubes and salad oil.

WHO WRITES THIS STUFF?

THE LITERATI OF LINT

It is widely assumed that there are thousands of people across the globe huddled in think tanks with names like The June Cleaver Foundation whose job it is to formulate, test, evaluate, and then write up household hints for publication.

In fact, there are only three people who do this. They convene on Mondays and Thursdays, crack a couple of bottles of Boone's Farm, and lie around the living room in ratty bathrobes, painting their toenails and making things up.

This explains why so many household hints sound like they were written by three women in chenille sucking on cheap wine.

Writing household hints is like writing in any other genre; there are formulas and conventions that apply. When coming up with dandy tips and hints and tricks of the trade, these Three Women in Chenille religiously observe the following rules.

RULE NUMBER 1: **Never use a product specially formulated for the task.**

Household hints are predicated on using products that were designed with an entirely different use in mind. For example, if you wish to clean your oven, you must never use Oven Cleaner. Try a hair grooming product or, better yet, a high-potency vitamin supplement.

The now-defunct can of oven cleaner need not go to waste, either. It is an effective, budget-conscious alternative to expensive medically supervised wart

removals and a handy substitute for bikini-line depila-
tories.

RULE NUMBER 2: **Never buy a product when you can
make it at home in just one afternoon from products
already on hand or available at any livery stable, at a
cost of just 9 or 10 times what you would pay in a
store.**

The purchase of household products is the refuge
of the weak and lazy. Domestically Gifted people *make*
their own cleaning products.

Normal household effluvium can provide the basis
for hundreds of cleaning agents—a search through old
purses, the vegetable crisper, medicine chest, or crawl
space is like a trip to Wal-Mart.

For example, did you know that you can make a
dandy furniture polish from cigarette ashes, toothpaste, coffee grounds, linseed oil, pulverized walnut
meats, and owl droppings? Or that you can make your
own soap by stockpiling meat fat in the fridge until
you have enough to boil down with lye in a cast-iron
vat that you might have sitting around the living
room?

RULE NUMBER 3: **All homemade cleaning products
and techniques must make a bigger mess than the
original mess you're trying to clean up.**

A perfect example of this rule is the classic Pea-
nut-Butter Remedy for removing chewing gum from a
child's hair. Slather a good cup or so of Skippy
(Smooth or Chunky) into your little one's tresses. Pat
her on the bottom and send her off to play near the
bird feeder. In an hour or so, most of her hair will be

gone and, along with it, that pesky chewing gum.

RULE NUMBER 4: All household hints must be written as if the reader had the IQ of guava jelly and such that improper implementation could result in a lawsuit.
It must be assumed that, even though the reader possesses enough intelligence to actually read the household hint, she is actually a drooling idiot with the intelligence of Noxzema—evidenced by the fact that she is occupying her time with household hints. She will however, be a crack expert in matters of product liability law. Consequently, a hint on ironing will take the following form:

"Before beginning any ironing task, it is recommended that you have a complete physical and Pap smear. Then, after a licensed, bonded electrician has checked out the wiring in your home, plug in the iron, being sure you are properly clothed in insulated footwear and protective goggles. Take care that there are no children or pets within a five-state area! Avoid setting up the ironing board in standing water or storm drains, and never iron anything that might melt, such as butter, dry cleaning bags, or marshmallows."

RULE NUMBER 5: All household hints must reject the use of modern technology.
Purists believe that, to be valid, a bona fide Household Hint cannot avail itself of anything invented after 1903. For example, the proper way to clean a broiler pan will involve making a paste of fish scales, baking soda, and aged cheese, which is applied vigorously with a swatch of burlap that has been soaked in kero-

sene and dried in a kiln. Using a two-cent scouring pad is out of the question.

RULE NUMBER 6: **The only time-saving hints that can be offered are those that save time on tasks nobody does anyway.**

For example, you will encounter such time-saving gems as: "Save time and effort! Clean and wax the numbers on your appliance dials by removing them from the stove and tying them to the front bumper of the car before you take it through the car wash."

RULE NUMBER 7: **Good time-saving hints must be embarrassing to implement.**

Most time-saving hints operate by combining tasks that are seldom performed together except in the circus or among people suffering from a chemical imbalance.

While you may indeed save time by consolidating breadcrumb-crushing with step aerobics at the YMCA, the time needed for explanation to wary onlookers more than negates the gain. And yes, one *can* treat a headache, entertain the kiddies, and thaw dinner at the same time by sitting with a frozen leg of lamb on your head. Should you actually decide to do this, make sure the curtains are closed.

RULE NUMBER 8: **The proper household hint presupposes an unlimited availability of time and a clear inability to discern the proper use thereof.**

Typical are instructions such as how to save and then melt down all your soap slivers in a double boiler in order to produce one large algae-colored lump for a decorative accent in the guest bathroom that resembles something deposited by a large rodent with intestinal problems. Sure to brighten up any bathroom.

RULE NUMBER 9: Household hints need not always be bizarre. Common sense can be a surprising source of household hints.

When the writers of household hints run out of uses for cream of tartar in the nursery, or if they just wish to knock off work early, they may resort to such startling revelations as: "Ink stains on shirts are messy and difficult to remove, but they *can be avoided* by keeping all pens in a desk drawer."

RULE NUMBER 10: Household hints should purport to either save money or save the planet.

Because most household hints are such a pain in the asphalt to implement, they must offer financial or ecological incentives to justify the extraordinary inconvenience and often unattractive results involved. In practice, however, the savings must work out to be less than the cost of implementing the idea, and the ecological benefit must be unprovable. This rule is borrowed from appropriations committees of the United States Congress and is the basis for many bestselling books written by vice presidents.

ACTUAL REAL-LIFE, HONEST-TO-GOD TRUE EXAMPLES OF PUBLISHED HOUSEHOLD HINTS

Yes, Virginia, there are idiots out there, and they're trying to tell *you* how to be a better homemaker.

Here are a few household hints, directly from the

pages of magazines and books *actually sold in this country*—written by the Three Women in Chenille, who, alarmingly, also vote and bear children. In the interest of science and mental health, following each item is a common-sense analysis, because you have a right to know the unvarnished truth about Household Hints.

RECIPE FOR HOMEMADE TOOTHPASTE: **Scrape the charcoal from burnt toast and crush it to a fine powder. Reduce an equal amount of dried sage leaves to a powder. Dip a moistened toothbrush in the mixture to clean teeth.** This is probably an old folk recipe from impoverished rural areas in Arkansas, where efficient removal of black stuff lodged between one's teeth is not a concern due to the random nature of tooth placement among the inhabitants. Presumably it is the abrasive quality of blackened toast scrapings and pulverized weeds that cleans the tooth enamel. So if you are fresh out of sage and your toaster is working properly, you might try Comet.

SUNBURN REMEDY: **Whipped egg whites and castor oil.** This is a particularly handy hint for people who sunbathe in the company of lemon meringue pies. With egg whites already at their fingertips, they need only locate the medicine chest of someone with a regularity problem and voilà! edible Solarcaine.

LIP BALM RECIPE: **Spermaceti, beeswax, honey, and sweet almond oil melted in a double boiler.** Most people with functioning gag reflexes make a point of avoiding lip salves whose first ingredient is an Italian contraceptive. However, if you're not the queasy sort, and you happen to be a beekeeper and have on hand some particularly juicy almonds for squeezing, this can be a pleasant little project for, say, the entire month of August. Or you can buy a tube of Chap Stick for about seventy-nine cents.

HOMEMADE HAIRSPRAY: **Chop a whole lemon, cover with water in a saucepan, and boil the mixture until the liquid reduces by half. Strain the liquid through cheesecloth and add lavender water. Store in the fridge.** Assuming your supermarket stocks lavender water and cheesecloth, and you had the foresight to acquire them at an earlier time, this is a remarkably useful recipe. It is best kept on hand for those annoying little national emergencies such as those times when the entire supply of hairspray has been looted from store shelves by hordes of crazed country western singers and roving gangs of televangelists.

No time to shampoo? Brush oatmeal through your hair to remove dirt and oils. If, after looking at the picture of the Quaker Oats man on the box, you still wish to try this, bear in mind that the creators of this tip did not intend for you to use *cooked* oatmeal. In fact, this little nuance of interpretation was the basis for an entire episode of "I Love Lucy." (Caution: The current spokesperson for Quaker Oats is Wilford Brimley, who is bald.)

Cucumber peels mixed with salt will repel ants. Unfortunately, it only repels ants from the spot where you've piled this stuff. Consequently, you will be forced to have little vegetable-peel haystacks piled every six inches around your house. They will then rot into a slimy mess that will also repel *you.* (See chapter on cucumber stain removal.)

Set out pans of beer in your garden to get rid of slugs. This actually does work. The slugs are attracted to the beer, slither in headfirst, become intoxicated, and drown. Unfortunately, carousing bands of drunken garden pests singing off-key renditions of "Danny Boy" in the wee hours of the morning are likely to irritate the neighbors. *Note:* This is only effective with *garden* slugs. Pans of beer set about in the house will attract the Domestic Slug, also known as the Suburban Couch Potato Pest (Latin name: husbandus horizontalus), which is much harder to get rid of. If you wish to effectively repel these pests, you must set out pans of panty hose soaking in sudsy water.

Leather furniture can be cleaned with stale beer. This is why leather furniture is often the bachelor's decor of choice, working much the same way as a self-cleaning oven. Merely select the proper setting (napping; with beer can resting on belly) and let the scrubbing bubbles do the rest. (*Warning:* See previous hint on the Couch Potato Pest.)

Control mice with a mixture of cornmeal and cement placed in their feeding areas. This method not only controls the little critters, it kills them. *Bonus:* The now-deceased mice make unusual, one-of-a-kind paperweights for holiday gift giving.

For homemade glue, mix isinglass with nitric acid and soft water in a double boiler. Should you ever wake up one morning and find that federal agents have confiscated your stockpile of school glue, this is the recipe to have. First, you'll need to get a bunch of isinglass, found at fine isinglass stores everywhere. Or just haul on down to the creek and catch a mess of catfish, gut the air bladders (you knew that's where isinglass came from, didn't you?), invite the Culligan man, and boil 'em up with any nitric acid you might have left over from those recent pitch-in suppers with the IRA. What could be simpler?

Hair dyes can be made by boiling onion skins and black walnut skins or, for blondes, using boiled rhubarb roots. Should you ever find yourself stranded in the wilderness, hopelessly lost and foraging for roots and berries, it's good to know that you can still look good for that Associated Press photographer when you are rescued. Be sure that the wilderness you select provides access to cooking utensils, rubber gloves, and an electrical outlet for your blow-dryer.

Remove mildew smells from old trunks by scrubbing with mustard. The rationale for this hint is that the odor of mustard is more pleasant than the odor of mildew. Presumably one should use Grey Poupon if it is a very good steamer trunk from Europe. You may remove mustard smells from old trunks by scrubbing with any abrasive condiment, such as what you might find crusted in the screw-on caps of jars found in the back of your fridge.

Clean dirty wallpaper by rubbing slices of white bread over soiled areas. For centuries, homemakers have struggled with the problem of how to clean wallpaper; smearing food on it was the logical solution. It is most effective if the bread is not buttered first, and operates under the premise that anything white rubbed across a dirty surface will itself become dirty, giving the impression that actual cleaning takes place. Consequently, wedding gowns and sanitary napkins work equally well.

Polish tin by rubbing with a sliced onion. Actually, the onion does not polish the tin; its odor merely keeps people from getting close enough to see if it's polished or not. It also keeps them at a sufficient distance that they just might think the item is silver.

Out of copper polish? Try ketchup! In fact, the next time you take your family to McDonald's, why not take along a suitcase full of those neglected copper pots and plumbing fittings? Gather round the condiment station for a wholesome evening of buffing and burnishing! Tuck away a few extra packets for those last-minute copper polishing emergencies on the go.

Clean piano keys and bring out the shine with yogurt. Of course, "Heart and Soul" will never sound the same again, especially if you use the fruit-on-the-bottom kind. But the dazzling shine on those keys is well worth the artistic sacrifice, and the added calcium reduces osteoporosis in older upright pianos.

One of the best ways to polish brass is with Worcestershire sauce. This was discovered by military personnel after a lengthy investigation of soldiers charged with sexual harassment for making lewd advances to superior officers with a bottle of Lea & Perrins.

Rid your hands of paint odors by rubbing them with a freshly cut onion. The theory is simple: Cover up the stench with something stenchier. This, coincidentally, is the basis for much of the personal hygiene employed by people who stand in front of you in checkout lines and accounts for the success of products such as Aqua Velva. For household purposes, however, the same end result may be achieved by rubbing your hands with cat food or spoiled pork.

Polish leather shoes with the inside of a banana skin. Because of the brilliant sheen banana gunk imparts to your shoes, people will hardly notice that cloud of gnats swarming about your ankles when you walk into the board meeting. *Note:* The application of fruit to one's shoes is best done in the privacy of your own home.

MORE TRUE-LIFE EXAMPLES
OF PUBLISHED HOUSEHOLD HINTS
CONCOCTED BY PEOPLE
WHO HAVE NO LIVES

WITH CRITICAL ANALYSIS
BY SOMEONE WITH A LIFE

Candles will last longer if they are coated with shellac. For an additional hour's burning time on a 19-cent candle, you will spend:

- 15 minutes locating a can of shellac in the garage

- 32 minutes trying to get back into the house after locking yourself out

- 11 minutes locating a screwdriver to pry the can open

- 2 hours, 9 minutes at the emergency room after gouging your wrist with the screwdriver

- 1 hour, 12 minutes cleaning up (with one hand) the now-dried shellac that spattered on countertop and appliances while you were prying the can open and gouging your wrist

- 1 hour, 15 minutes taking family out to dinner since the kitchen stinks too much to cook in. Cost: $42.95 + tip

Unsightly dark extension cords against white walls can be made to match by painting the cords white. The same effect can also be achieved by purchasing white cords to begin with.

Save money by saving plastic newspaper sleeves for reuse as sandwich bags. This is not a bad idea if you don't mind washing these things and having to look at them draped all over everything til they dry, which takes approximately 40 days and 40 nights. However, your children will not want to be seen in the school lunchroom with sandwiches swathed in orange, water-spotted cellophane, so they will just throw them in the bushes before the bus comes. Yes, you could save

79 cents per year by doing this; or save $150 per year by cancelling the newspaper.

Keep moths away with saucers of tobacco or horse chestnuts. Not only will this keep moths away, it will keep away anything else with a functioning sense of smell, such as your family and friends. You can achieve the same results by hanging Limburger cheese in your closet. (See previous notations re: Aqua Velva.)

When washing fine woolen sweaters, stitch the buttonholes together first to prevent them from stretching out. This also provides hours of amusement watching Grandpa trying to put on his sweater.

Clean off the dryer lint screen with a baby-bottle brush. When the brush is later used to clean nursery bottles, this serves as an excellent way to introduce baby to solids. If baby is not ready for new foods, you can clean the bottle brush with a toothbrush. The toothbrush can then be cleaned with a mascara brush that has first been soaked overnight in a jar of ammonia. The jar then can be cleaned quickly and easily with a clean baby bottle brush.

Hard-to-reach cobwebs on the ceiling? Cover a helium-filled balloon with panty hose (sprayed with furniture polish), let the balloon rise, and good-bye cobwebs! This is a wonderful family project. First, locate a circus or a child's birthday party. Then abscond with a suitably perky balloon. Bring it back home and draw the drapes.

Then spend an afternoon attempting to shove it into a pair of Queen-Sized Sheer Energy Light Support panty hose. Spray with Endust, then release the balloon. It will immediately rise and go directly toward the nearest light fixture, where it will pop and give you all a heart attack. Or, because you forgot to tie a string to it, it will rise and stay on the ceiling forever and you will have to explain to visitors why there's a pair of panty hose hanging from your ceiling.

To eliminate bloodstains, sprinkle garment with meat tenderizer before laundering, and stains will disappear. The idea for this came from the kitchen of a maximum security prison, where inmates were encouraged to develop skills they could use on the outside. According to Rocco "The Butcher" Corleone, this helpful household hint also saves time—in Rocco's case, 20–40 years.

14
Getting Real
Tips from the Trenches

PRACTICAL, LITTLE-KNOWN
HOUSEHOLD TIPS YOU CAN REALLY USE

Most household hints require you to actually Perform Work, which pretty much defeats the general idea of household hints. A survey of some of the world's laziest people reveals some truly helpful tips:

• Hate dusting? It will be over before you know it if you simply wear a terry-cloth robe while making love on the dining room table. (*Hint:* Try a provocative spritz of Lemon Pledge. To avoid buildup, make love less frequently.)

• Panty hose make excellent dust cloths as well. Take care not to hurt your back as you lift your leg onto the mantel!

• A leaf blower makes quick work of those large dusting jobs, such as the entire first floor. Be sure to open windows before tackling this task. (*Bonus:* A leaf blower makes a great industrial-strength hair dryer for visiting TV anchorpersons.)

• Cleaning knickknacks need not be tedious and time-consuming. Simply fill the bathtub with hot, sudsy water. Place all bric-a-brac into an old pillowcase, tie it shut, and throw it into the trash. Relax in the hot bath, knowing you'll never have to clean that tacky stuff again.

• Remove stubborn ground-in stains from your children's play clothes simply and easily by packing them all up in the kids' overnight bag when they go to visit Grandma. The clothes will come back good as new (and may, in fact, actually *be* new).

• Get your kids to help out with housework by warning them that they are not, under *any circumstances*, to disturb the dust on the furniture by wiping it with that cloth you've left sitting on the counter. And if they so much as TOUCH that broom. . . !

• Avoid leaf raking by locating new subdivisions with "sunswept" lots and posting a sign saying: HOME-GROWN LEAVES FOR OLD-FASHIONED PILING AND JUMPING. FREE FOR THE TAKING. CALL 555-1212.

• Don't wash that kitchen floor! Tell everyone that the dull, sticky surface is a new space-age traction polymer that was recently applied (at great expense) for its safety benefits to your grandmother—who, you might add, broke her hip falling on her other, *selfish* granddaughter's newly waxed floor.

* Explain to visitors that, no, those are not cobwebs. You are making homemade cotton candy for the school fair.

* Never again bother with cleaning hard-water stains and soap scum from tubs and shower stalls. Merely wait until the deposit is approximately a half-inch thick, then, with an X-Acto knife, carve in beautiful designs such as swans, butterflies, and lilies. One enterprising young woman carried out her Early American motif with a detailed etching of an American eagle along with the entire text of the Declaration of Independence.

* Piles of dirty laundry in your kids' rooms, on the bathroom floor, or in the dining room can be passed off as room decor by calling it soft sculpture. *Bonus:* This may qualify for a grant from the National Endowment for the Arts.

HONEST ANSWERS TO
FREQUENTLY ASKED QUESTIONS

Q. *Must I always wear rubber gloves when cleaning?*

A. If you are using chemicals obtained from Superfund landfills and wish to avoid the inconvenience and expense of skin grafts, yes, it is advisable. If you're simply dusting or picking up, you can forego the gloves. (However, if you're tidying up after burglarizing your neighbor's house, you might want to consider the advantages offered by rubber gloves, such as preventing those annoying latent prints.)

Q. *What's the best way to transport a Jell-O mold without damaging it?*

A. Now, this question illustrates perfectly why this country is in major decline. Why do you *care* about damaging it? It's mold! There is no point in transporting mold at all. Just throw the whole thing away.

Q. *I have a problem with sticky drawers. What's the best way to alleviate this problem?*

A. Perhaps you have too much fiber in your diet. See a good internist.

Q. *Is there any way to prevent mildew from forming in the tile grout of the shower stall?*

A. Yes. Mildew requires both warmth and moisture in order to grow. Therefore, you should keep the temperature in your bathroom at about 34°F and avoid turning on the water spigots while in the shower.

Q. *What is the best method for cleaning a septic tank?*

A. Why would you bother cleaning anything into which you're going to put sewage? It's OK for a septic tank to be filthy; it's *designed* to store filth. Relax! Who looks in there anyway?

Q. *What is the best way to keep plaster lawn ornaments looking good?*

A. Other than wrapping them in several thicknesses of insulation batting and storing them in your attic, there is no way that plaster lawn ornaments will ever look good.

Q. *Is there any way to speed up the process of defrosting a freezer?*

A. Yes! Using a chain saw or electric knife is helpful. Be sure to wear welder's goggles, since flying shards of ice lodged in the cornea are unsightly and painful. The time will pass more quickly if you amuse yourself by carving intricate designs into the ice. You can satisfy your creative urges while curtailing your kids' between-meal raids on the Klondike bars by sculpting a grotesque display of gargoyles in the freezer compartment and telling them the Frigidaire is possessed.

Q. *When using cotton swabs to clean the scrollwork on the architectural molding on the exterior of the house, is it best to work from bottom up or top down?*

A. It depends upon the architectural style. Doric should be done from top down, Ionic should be done from bottom up, and Corinthian from side to side. However, since you asked this question, you might wish to check with your psychiatrist to determine whether you should be on a ladder at all.

READERS WRITE IN

FLASHES OF BRILLIANCE
FROM ORDINARY PEOPLE

On occasion, the Three Women in Chenille decide they don't feel like writing any household hints today. So they turn over their columns to contributions sent in by readers from all over the country, many of whom appear to have not yet caught up with the news that the Allies won the war.

Consequently, you'll read helpful hints such as these.

Dear Women in Chenille,

I have several friends, and remembering all their phone numbers and addresses was becoming confusing. The telephone directory does not match the mushroom wallpaper in my kitchen, and also contains too many numbers of people I don't remember. It was very time-consuming to have to sort through all those names. So what I did was buy a little book at the store that had alphabetical tabs! I then wrote the names and numbers of my friends in this book, putting each person under the tab that most closely matched the first letter of their last name. (You can cover it with Con-Tact paper to match your kitchen, too!) I keep it by the phone, and it's now a simple matter to find a friend's phone number any time I want.

Sincerely,
Delighted Diane, Dialing
Direct

Dear Women in Chenille,

I had struggled for years with the frustrating task of finding the end of the plastic wrap on the roll, until one day I discovered that you can leave a little bit of the end hanging out of the box. Next time you need to wrap something, PRESTO! There it is! I have shared this with my friends, and they are all amazed at how clever I am.

Sincerely,
Marilyn in Mahtomedi

Dear Women in Chenille,

While making homemade goat-milk cottage cheese one day, I got rung up by my neighbor, says she wants my breeding bull out of her flower bed. Petunias they was. I left the kitchen for a short spell (she only lives four miles upriver from the old abandoned mine), but when I come back, I seen the whole house was in flames. So I'm writing in to warn readers that they shouldn't leave their cottage cheese on the stove unattended, least while their breeding bull's in season.

Sincerely,
Homeless in Montana

Dear Women in Chenille,

Always looking for ways to recycle and save the earth, I was delighted to discover yet another use for discarded pistachio shells. Many are just the right size and shape to substitute in a pinch for a broken fingernail. Just glue on and go! The red pistachios even save you time with nail polish and *are lots less expensive than artificial nails. Unless you have been a recent game show contestant and received a year's supply of Lee Press-On Nails as one of your fabulous parting gifts, you'll appreciate the $7.99/lb price tag for up to 300 nails.*

Sincerely,
Distinctive Digits in Denver

Dear Women in Chenille,

Like most women, I was at my wit's end trying to keep coordinating hankies for each of my 424 outfits organized and ready to go. I found that by removing all of my husband's clothes from the bureau and closets, and relocating them to a rental storage unit not far from our house, there was plenty of room to properly arrange my hankies for easy access. It's amazing the storage we can find right in our own homes!

Sincerely,
Glamorous Gloria

Dear Women in Chenille,

After countless visits to the emergency room with cut feet from broken glass left on my floor after all-night drunken parties, I discovered that if I poured the tequila into plastic cups, my friends could smash their glasses against the wall with little or no cleanup the next day. I got to thinking that your readers might be able to use this little hint.

Sincerely,
Domestic Dale

Dear Women in Chenille,

If you're like me, you might want to do something wacky, like have a big dinner on Thanksgiving. I have found that turkey goes over quite well on such occasions. You can find them in your grocer's frozen food case, and many of them already come stuffed with something, although it does not resemble Stove Top stuffing. Just remember to thaw the turkey and to turn on the oven well ahead of when your guests arrive.

Sincerely,
Newlywed in Newport News

Dear Women in Chenille,

With seven children and one on the way, plus school activities, Brownies, Boy Scouts, and church, I don't have the time to deal with trivial things like regular sex with my husband. Imagine my delight when I discovered that there are women out there who will do this for as little as $10 per hour! Sure freed up a lot of my time! You may have printed this hint before, but it was a new one to me, and I thought I should send it in for other harried moms.

Sincerely,
Overjoyed in Opelika

15
Artsy Phartsy
Cutesy Crafts to Make You Puke

THE WOMANLY ART OF MAKING JUNK

What do you see when you look at a pile of sticky Popsicle sticks stuck to the glass-topped coffee table? Do you see a Big Fat Mess? Do you see yourself reaching for the Windex while muttering obscenities under your breath?

BZZZZZZ! *Wrong answer.* Error error error. The *correct* answer, for all you good little homemakers, is that you see the makings of an entire pioneer village, circa 1816.

Any homemaker worth her refrigerator magnets must be skilled in the art of craftsy kitsch, wherein junk is magically transformed—through feminine creative nurturing skills—into breathtaking Home Decor.

No one is saying just *whose* home this is considered decor in, but this stuff will, without question, take your breath away, albeit in short, labored gasps.

It is no coincidence that crafts have long been used in therapy groups for the criminally insane. But do not let this stigma cause you undue concern; crafts have now gone mainstream and are openly practiced without shame by millions of people, most of whom deliberately misspell their first names by changing the final *y* ending into an *i* (which they dot with a smiley face), e.g., Nanci, Cindi, Kelli, Gadhafi.

So if you wish to be accepted in Domestically Gifted circles, start thinking *CUTE*.

OVERCOMING YOUR NATURAL AVERSION TO TACKY ITEMS IN YOUR HOME

Being artsy craftsy is, of course, a requirement for membership into that sisterhood known as the Domestically Gifted. However, except in the case of genetic disorders, people are not born with an instinctive urge to create faux Byzantine mosaics out of Lee Press-On Nails.

They must be indoctrinated and taught.

This is why so many "women's" magazines are chock-full of propaganda articles that lead the casual observer to believe that all women have incredible amounts of time on their hands that are best filled by making stuffed snakes out of their husbands' old neckties or dressing up the Mrs. Butterworth syrup bottle.

Sadly, too many women today have neither the time nor the inclination to fashion frilly frocks for the syrup bottle. Most normal women, ashamed to admit that they fail to understand the value of such pursuits, then feel guilty about their obvious domestic deficiencies.

You will notice, however, in photo layouts of gorgeous homes in these *same magazines,* that you seldom see Mrs. Butterworth atop the mantel modeling her latest outfit. Nor will you find feathered and bejeweled fly-swatter covers, bottle-top picture frames, or windows graced with valances made from garbage bags and panty hose.

The truth is they're trying to trick you into trashing your lovely home with these tacky projects so that *their* homes will look terrific in comparison.

HOW TO RECOGNIZE A TACKY MOTIF

If your considered craft item incorporates any of the following, it's bona fide tacky:

- plastic butterflies

- grinning frogs (Steuben glass frogs are OK.)

- little girls with huge eyes and huge bonnets

- elves reclining under mushrooms

- Elvis (reclining under a mushroom or otherwise)

ANTHROPOMORPHISM AND YOU

Do you have little hausfrau geese in babushkas and aprons waddling across the wainscoting of your kitchen? How about ceramic humanoid frogs? No kitchen is complete without an amphibian in a three-piece suit lounging around the sink area with a soap pad stuffed in its mouth.

It's not enough that your crafts be cute; they must

attribute human qualities to inanimate objects or members of the animal kingdom. You know you're on the right track if your home resembles the dust jacket of *Wind in the Willows*.

Start with woodland creatures. Animals that are repugnant in their natural state become Home Decor when replicated in plastic, plaster, or ceramic and made to wear clothing appropriate for church services. Is there nothing more precious than a mole in his Sunday best? (If you cannot locate a religious mole, a nattily dressed agnostic will do.)

As you become more sophisticated at this, you will want to expand into other forms of woodland life, such as the beloved mushrooms. All artsy-craftsy kitchens must be littered with mass quantities of air fresheners masquerading as fungi.

Paint, sew, or glue eyes on everything! A well-decked house has observant, watchful furniture and accesories, especially in the nursery. Clocks are especially good for this, since they already have hands, and can be made to look relatively human in just an afternoon. You should, of course, address these items by name—Mr. Clock, Mrs. Potty Chair, Herr Brush.

THE SEXUAL POLITICS OF CRAFTS

When a man makes something, it is *handcrafted*, a term that evokes the image of a skilled artisan (heavy on the testosterone, with a strong jaw, craggy face, muscular arms all carved out and bulgy, and drop-dead gorgeous, sensitive blue eyes that whisper, "I want you").

When a woman makes something, it is *homemade*, a term that paints a homespun picture of quaint, make-do charm, involving sturdy women with rosy cheeks wearing Xtra large Carter's cotton briefs. The item this woman makes is usually described as "darling."

Men, on the other hand, do not make Darling Things. They make Handsome, Heirloom-quality Keepsakes (spoken *basso profundo*). They do not make things out of milk cartons, toilet tissue cardboard, or dryer lint. They create Lasting Works of Functional Beauty from mahogany, oak, or precious metals.

Men are *craftsmen*. It's a title—like Knight, Duke, or Sire—intended to bestow stature. Women, on the other hand, are *crafty*, a term normally used in the context of wicked witches and state hospital escapees who've managed to evade capture.

DIFFERENTIATING BETWEEN HANDCRAFTED ITEMS AND HOMEMADE CRAFTS

• If you can imagine it on the bulletin board at Kindercare or in the home of a neighbor who dresses up her parakeet for Memorial Day parades, it's probably a Homemade Craft.

• If it required the purchase of 11 power tools and a case of Budweiser, it's Handcrafted.

• If the only thing you can think to say about it involves a high-pitched squeal and the word *how* followed by *cute, clever, adorable, precious,* or *darling,* it's a Homemade Craft.

• If its construction necessitated leaving every window in the house open for "proper ventilation," it's Handcrafted.

A WORD ABOUT MEN AND RUFFLES, BOWS, FLOUNCES, AND LACE

Many women have been led to believe that a warm, homey atmosphere can only be created with the addition of mass quantities of sissy stuff. This is known as the Feminine Touch. Unfortunately, many women apply the same subtle touch to decorating that Mike Tyson applies to courtship.

Instead of achieving the desired effect of showcasing competent homemaking skills, the place looks like an explosion in the little girl's Easter Dress Department of K mart.

Most men do not feel comfortable around such things. They will not feel warm and cozy and nurtured and grateful to have such a fine little wifey. They will be *pissed* that they have to plow through tulle and lace and eyelet to find you under the covers, and they'll be *really* honked off when they find their fishing box covered with seed pearls.

They might tolerate such things in the kitchen, considering that area yours anyway. They view ruffles and bows in the kitchen as a form of territorial marking—the marital version of a rutting moose marking its tree. They understand wilderness hunter-gatherer-type stuff. But if you value your relationship at all, cutesy in the family room is out.

Inexplicably, men do not like to set about cleaning and oiling their guns in rooms apparently decorated by elves and fairies and filled with hundreds of teensy little glass mice with teensy little beady eyes peering out from what used to be a gun case.

Most men feel that masses of teensy print pastel fabrics gathered and crimped and shirred and flounced about windows, furniture, and lampshades are not compatible with the ESPN experience.

Watching the Vikings kick ass on Monday Night Football is somehow not as satisfying with a Laura Ashley window treatment draped and poufed about the TV screen. The only yardage they want to see involves running backs. To people with facial and chest hair, net yardage does not mean nylon net puff balls or lampshades made to look like ballerina tutus.

Avoid the following items in the vicinity of TVs, game rooms, or workbenches:

• crocheted beer can cozies

• doily coasters

• windchimes

• Precious Moments figurines

   Do not:

• Stencil geese wearing bonnets anywhere near a cable TV outlet

• Stitch needlepoint slipcovers for the remote control

• Make smiley faces on the nacho chips with the cheese sauce

• Tuck Ukrainian egg people into the pool table pockets

ECOLOGICALLY RESPONSIBLE
DECORATING WITH CRAFTS

Up until recently, most interior designers generally agreed that the first rule of thumb was: "Try not to decorate your home with things made from items dug from your trash compactor."

The reasoning was, of course, that if it deserved to go in there, it doesn't deserve to be on your sofa, on your windows, or on your head.

Then, one day, the Head Interior Design Maven of the World incurred a massive head injury that caused her to make placemats from junked Yugo floormats and a pair of pinking shears. Suddenly, her favorite fabric designer was "Hefty."

This caught on, and recycling fanatics everywhere (many of whom suffer from brain injuries of their own) began chanting, "One man's trash is another man's treasure!" Fine. Just make sure *your* rubbish reincarnates itself as a toss pillow on *their* sofa.

Here are some trendy ideas for decorating your home with items that would otherwise clog a landfill:

• Used disposable diapers are wonderful for window-box seedling starts. The natural fertilizer provides an excellent growth medium.

• Empty aluminum beverage cans can be flattened and used as coasters for other aluminum drink containers. Coordinate same-brand cans for an especially chic effect. Or mix and match for a bit of whimsy!

• Plastic yogurt cups covered with felt make dandy last-minute dice cups for those spontaneous all-neighborhood Yahtzee parties.

• Don't throw out those chicken bones! Wash and lay them out in the sun to bleach. If your dog doesn't choke on them first, you can use them to make little politically correct Christmas ornaments. The wishbones make cunning little bow-legged angels, sure to bring a smile to the face of any child suffering from rickets.

16
You Too Can Be Artsy Phartsy
How-Tos for Those Who Oughtn't

CRAFTS EVEN YOU CAN DO

Since you are Domestically Impaired, it's best to stay away from craft magazines. You wouldn't begin to be able to understand the intricate directions and procedures involved in transforming freezer frost, poison oak, and dryer lint into fabulous centerpieces. However, if you have mastered rudimentary large motor skills and feel compelled to express your creative side, there are some exciting projects from Actual Craft Publications that can be adapted to even your level of incompetence.

WHAT THEY SUGGEST: Beautify your bedroom by making your own romantic, designer toss pillows. Stuff an old satin and lace slip with discarded panty hose, gather up at the ends, and tie with a pretty ribbon.

WHAT YOU SHOULD DO: Beautify your bedroom by gathering up your old slips and panty hose off the floor and stuff them into a drawer. Tie the drawer shut with a pretty ribbon.

WHAT THEY SUGGEST: Make unusual napkin rings from old spoons. Heat the metal and bend into a circle, and then pound out into the shape you want.

WHAT YOU SHOULD DO: Save yourself a lot of trouble by inviting Uri Geller to dinner.

WHAT THEY SUGGEST: Have beautiful, expensive flooring at a fraction of the price with the magic of trompe l'oeil. Merely paint on a realistic-looking marble finish or intricate Spanish tile.

WHAT YOU SHOULD DO: For a really realistic floor, paint on Kool-Aid stains, tennis shoes, doggy accidents, and Legos.

WHAT THEY SUGGEST: Your family will love waking up to personalized toast! Spread peanut butter or their favorite jam over a plastic stencil bearing their names or a cheery message, positioned over toasted bread. Carefully remove stencil, and voilà! designer toast.

WHAT YOU SHOULD DO: No more early morning arguing over whose toast is whose! Start by burning your toast as usual. Then carefully position blackened toast over the sink and, with a sharp knife, carve each family member's favorite Druid marking into the carbon. Or, for a bit of whimsy, how about a personal message? How Grandma will beam when her very own toast bids her a cheery day with the words *Helter Skelter.*

BEFORE YOU BEGIN

Many suggested craft projects involve turning something presentable into something junky. Now *junky*, as used here, is a technical term. It is not meant to impugn the tastes of persons who consider a hot glue gun and macaroni the equivalent of a degree in interior design. It's merely trade jargon used among such professionals as you might find in the Craft Therapy room of the state hospital. Experienced crafters know what to look for when assessing potential junkiness. You'll want to be on the lookout for projects that:

- Require 10 coats of polyurethane, particularly clocks and inspirational sayings on amoeba-shaped pieces of wood

- Use felt, glitter, or marabou feathers

- Combine velour and fluorescent paint in any manner

- Require you to save up empty panty-hose eggs

- Involve the likeness of Jesus in combination with batteries or neon

BAZAARS

ANYTHING THAT SOUNDS BIZARRE PROBABLY IS

You'll want to hang out with the movers and shakers in the glamorous, whirlwind scene of the Artsy Phartsy. The best places to do this are flea markets and bazaars, which are simply marketplaces to which you bring all your unsightly items and sell them to unsuspecting nearsighted people who spend their waking hours watching QVC. Many people do not know about flea markets and bazaars, which explains the brisk traffic at the Goodwill drop-off bin.

Do not be misled by the name *flea market*. There are no fleas sold at these places. However, if you're in the market for fleas, many of the items offered for sale will be infested with them, and the savvy shopper can spot those bargains by noting the general hygiene of the vendor.

For true artsy-phartsy items, which are actually homemade in actual homes with plumbing located in countries featured in an atlas, you'll want to go to a Bazaar.

Bazaars are flea markets that require the vendors to wear a shirt and to visit a dentist periodically.

The reason there are so many bazaars at Christmastime is because everyone's judgment is sufficiently impaired by champagne, wassail, and eggnog so as to be easily induced into believing that a spray-painted Pringle is now a Yuletide tree ornament for which they should pay $19.50.

BAZAAR CRAFT
INSTRUCTIONS AND WARNINGS

WHAT THEY SUGGEST: Tack about a hundred bottle caps upside down onto a doormat for scraping muddy boots.

ACTUAL RESULTS: Your next door neighbor's child will trip on it, slice open her shin, and sue you for umpteen kajillion dollars.

WHAT THEY SUGGEST: Dress up a picture frame for a cherished family photo by gluing on elbow macaroni shells and spray painting it gold.

ACTUAL RESULTS: It will look like an infestation of gaily costumed june bug larvae circling and preparing to attack your Aunt Clara's face.

WHAT THEY SUGGEST: Make a delightful toilet paper cozy by gluing eyes and a smiley face onto a potholder mitt to cover the extra roll sitting atop the toilet tank.

ACTUAL RESULTS: Not only will some poor schmuck have to undergo years of counseling to overcome being watched by a leering oven mitt during his constitutional, he's unlikely to guess where you've hidden the replacement roll—necessitating the use of your guest towel.

WHAT THEY SUGGEST: Make gift brooches and tie tacks from dried beans, lentils, and tapioca beads.

ACTUAL RESULTS: Unless the recipient of this gift normally buys her clothes in the frozen food section, she will probably not want to accessorize herself with items from the pantry. Besides, too few people have the fashion savvy to know how to judiciously mix cashmere and lima beans.

WHAT THEY SUGGEST: Add a delightful touch of amusing whimsy to the powder room by hanging a wooden spoon you've decorated with painted faces.

ACTUAL RESULTS: Most guests prefer to get their ration of whimsy in more festive places than your bathroom, and will undoubtedly discuss you in great detail at the next neighborhood party.

A TREASURE TROVE OF IDEAS
FROM YOUR GARBAGE

Lists of things to do with junk out of your trash are always given euphemistic names like Treasure Trove. Craft magazines found little interest in articles more truthfully entitled "A Rubbish Heap of Decorating Ideas for Your Son's Bar Mitzvah."

Cigarette Filters

• Great for packing and cushioning fragile stemware for shipping.

- Make unusual decorative mosaics with a variety of filters to give a stylish touch to those plain "no smoking" signs.

- Teach your little girl about the wonders of puberty with a doll-sized tampon.

Used Sandwich Bags

- Wonderful upholstery covers for dollhouse furniture in Barbie's Trailer Home.

- Great little oxygen tents for when the kids play Let's Pretend the Weebles Have Tuberculosis.

- Handy see-through garment bags for Robert Reich's suits.

Old Shower Caps

- Great props for when your kids play Rap Star, MD.

- Fill several with helium and tie shut with a long ribbon as a substitute for those expensive Mylar balloon bouquets.

- Starched heavily, these make great emergency substitutes for athletic supporters.

- Two sewn together make a dandy strapless bra for well-endowed women.

Empty Nondairy Creamer Containers from the Diner

- Great individual, purse-sized spittoons.

- Imagine the delight on your child's face when she sees her dollhouse equipped with miniature potty-training toilets!

- Turned upside down, they make perfect rose cones for landscaping the Fisher-Price village.

- Add an elegant touch to your formal dinner table with unique individual M&M servers.

- Surprise your child with adorable Ku Klux Klan finger puppets.

Pencil Shavings

- Great mulch for terrarium gardens.

- Save up and use as gerbil bedding.

- An acceptable substitute for bran in cooking.

Used Aluminum Foil

- Wad up into balls and stuff into a friend's carry-on bag before he goes through airport security.

- Large pieces can be shaped and formed into portable, lightweight lawn ornaments.

- Make a glitzy rain bonnet as a thoughtful gift for your husband's ex-wife during electrical storms.

- Elegant holiday toilet paper in your powder room.

Dryer Lint

- Great for stuffing toys or bras.

- White lint: wonderful for making Santa beards or Barbara Bush soft sculptures.

- Pink lint: tax-deductible attic insulation.

- Dark lint: paste onto underarms for that Madonna look.

CRAFTS FOR GIFT GIVING

PROVING IT IS ALWAYS BETTER
TO GIVE THAN TO RECEIVE

Many of the craft ideas circulating in books, magazines, and clubs were designed for gift giving, inasmuch as you would have to be clinically insane to keep the stuff in *your* house.

Homemade crafts always send a very special message to the recipient. Unfortunately, too often this message is, "I want your home to look like Graceland."

Some homemade items do send a loving message, however, and are universally well received. Anything handcrafted from real gold is always welcome, as are crafty items utilizing jade, diamonds, or rubies.

Giving away your crafts is, in fact, always a good idea. Let the recipient figure out how to dispose of the stuff.

PAWNING OFF YOUR
CRAFTS ON THE SENILE

CRIMES AGAINST THE ELDERLY

Possibly the cruelest thing artsy-craftsy people do is suggest that you make crafts for those hard-to-buy-for senior citizens on your gift list—as if arthritis and wrinkles weren't indignity enough for these dear old people. Apparently the theory is that receding gums and receding hairlines are universal symptoms for the onset of receding taste.

In the past, failing eyesight among the elderly has made them ideal targets for monstrously tacky projects—which is why seniors are so anxious to undergo cataract surgery.

It is evidently a mean streak that compels people to take the artsy-craftsy approach to senior gift giving, because the truth of the matter is, they don't want your junk any more than you do. If you are over the age of seven, Grandma and Grandpa *DO NOT WANT* your little projects. They are now at a stage in their lives where they can afford to decorate the way they have always wanted to ... which includes white carpeting, designer fabrics, and limited-edition lithographs. Never once did the words. *Popsicle-stick napkin holder* show up on their wish list. Pay attention to the following scenarios:

WHAT THEY SUGGEST: Those empty cardboard toilet-paper rolls can be covered with sequins, beads, and bits of lace to make charming Victorian pencil holders for Grandma's writing desk.

ANALYSIS: Unless Grandma has failing eyesight and delusions that she is Emily Dickinson, she is unlikely to appreciate gaudy clutter added to the mountainous stack of Medicare paperwork on her desk.

WHAT THEY SUGGEST: Cover discarded film canisters with faux pearls and dried flowers for an attractive alternative to ugly prescription medication bottles.

ANALYSIS: On her next trip to Acapulco, while racking up Frequent Flier mileage, Great-Grandma's purse will be confiscated by customs officials and she'll be charged with international drug smuggling.

WHAT THEY SUGGEST: Weave a cozy lap blanket from old flannel shirts to warm Grandpa's knees on chilly winter days.

ANALYSIS: On chilly winter days, Grandpa's more than likely going to be on the golf course somewhere in Arizona, and that cozy lap blanket will be used to clean his fairway irons.

WHAT THEY SUGGEST: Make clever shoe trees for Dad by stuffing an old sock with rolled newspaper and tying with pretty yarn.

ANALYSIS: Dear Old Dad is likely to name someone more competent to be executor of his estate.

WHAT THEY SUGGEST: Turn old pot holders into cozy slippers for an elderly aunt.

ANALYSIS: Great-Aunt Ginny prefers shopping at Foot Locker, and the pot-holder slippers are likely to be too bulky to wear with the Nike cross-trainers, anyway.

WHAT THEY SUGGEST: Grandparents will love displaying photos of the grandkids with a one-of-a-kind collage picture frame you make out of plastic six-pack carriers.

ANALYSIS: Grandma and Grandpa will look at each other and say, "For this we spent $50,000 putting her through college?"

17
Holiday Crafts
Tis the Season to Be Tacky

Holidays provide a great opportunity to indulge the primal urge to make stuff out of other, totally unrelated stuff. The seasonal nature of holidays ensures that your family and friends will not have to endure the sight of these crafty items for more than a few weeks.

CHRISTMAS

POMANDERS: Many people like to celebrate Christmas by making their clothes smell like an East Indian tea store. This is accomplished with the use of pomanders—oranges stuck with cloves that are hung up with a pretty ribbon. Now, customarily, it is not wise to hang perishable food in your closets. However, the act of tying food with a ribbon and hanging it amongst your woolens evidently functions as a preservative, and is just one of those Christmas miracles that defy explanation. The miracle does not apply to avocados, bananas, red meat, or poultry.

WREATHS: You can make a festive, welcoming holiday wreath out of just about anything, and if you check craft magazines, you will see that this is true. Try stuffing fistfuls of noxious weeds from a neighboring field into a grapevine wreath for a charming addition to the guest room you've prepared for Cousin Enid with the terrible allergies. Finish off with tufts of cat hair.

ADVENT CALENDARS: These are delightful little calendars that help your children count down to Christmas, building their anticipation to a fever pitch so that you have to scrape them off the ceiling with a sturdy spatula and go knocking on your neighbors' doors asking if you can borrow a cup of Ritalin.

LUMINARIES: These traditional paper-bag candle holders lead visitors to your house on dark evenings, where guests need only follow the flashing lights and blaring sirens of the fire trucks responding to the raging blaze caused by these quaint incendiary devices.

ORNAMENTS: The sentimental, warm feeling you get when looking at a tree decorated with homemade ornaments more than makes up for the really unattractive, overall flea-market effect. Parents of young children are likely to find their trees decorated with squashed soda cans, clothespins, and empty yogurt containers attempting to impersonate bells. (The teachers who teach them how to make this stuff all worked on the set of "Sanford and Son.")

EASTER

For centuries, people searched for an appropriate way to commemorate the most solemn holiday of Christianity. It was not until the twentieth century that theologians discovered that the proper way to observe Easter was with the lavish use of pink and pale purple cheap plastic items. This decorating scheme also served to secularize the holiday for people who objected to the religious connotations of Easter, such as the manufacturers of pink and pale purple cheap plastic items.

To further carry out the theme, it is recommended that you put rabbit ears and cotton bunny tails on everything and deposit plastic eggs on every conceivable surface. (Your husband will be delighted!) Add large amounts of fluorescent-colored plastic grass (grown on the hillsides of Chernobyl) and buy truckloads of brown candle wax sold as *imitation chocolate rabbits.* Put these in baskets and leave them lying everywhere. After Easter, insert a wick into the bunny's eye and save it for use in Christmas luminaries.

Color hard-boiled eggs so as to perpetuate the charming myth of magical egg-laying rabbits whose reproductive systems were evidently tampered with by Steven Spielberg.

Make Easter trees to complete the effect. Locate the scraggliest-looking tree in your front yard. Cover its bare branches with hundreds of panty-hose eggs that you've decorated in garish colors. Stand back and wait for admiring glances from the realtor who's trying to sell the house next door.

HALLOWEEN

This is the one holiday where tacky works. Because this holiday originated among people for whom chicken entrails constitute wall decor, no one expects Halloween to be tasteful. Black and orange crepe paper, plastic spiders, and paper witch hats are all considered haute couture . . . *for one day only.* On November 1, the bright orange leaf bags dotting your front lawn, black paper cats stuck to the window, and bed sheets hanging from the lamppost suddenly cause your home's market value to plummet.

Don't forget, of course, to carve your pumpkin! Smoldering vegetables on your front porch are Important Home Fashion. If you don't have one, you will learn about another decorative technique for your home called *egging.*

The best outlet for artsy-phartsy types during Halloween is making costumes. Magazines are full of complicated, involved projects that involve unsavory activities such as sewing.

But they also offer ideas for costumes that Even You Can Do. (The ideas will be contained in articles with condescending, guilt-inducing titles such as, "Last Minute, Hurry-Up Costumes for People Who Are Too Busy to Give of Themselves to Their Precious Little Ones.") They generally involve a pillowcase, garbage bag, or paper sack with eye holes; your child will throw himself on the floor sobbing as you instruct him how to make appropriate sound effects so people know what he's supposed to be.

Unfortunately, there is always some neighborhood mom who mucks up the works by stitching professional-caliber costumes for her entire family, making them look like the touring company of Disney on Ice.

So, while other children trick-or-treat in authentic period costumes from *A Man for All Seasons*, your little ones skulk from door to door as robots covered in used aluminum foil that still smells of tuna salad, sobbing, "Danger, Will Robinson!"

18
Time Management
H. G. Wells Meets Donna Reed

WHY YOU DON'T HAVE ENOUGH TIME

The hours in your day are not like the hours in other people's days.

Their 24 hours are composed of minutes, which occur in an orderly, predictable sequence, whereas *your* 24-hour day is composed of brief flashes of time, randomly dispersed and occurring without notice—like tax audits and visits from your mother-in-law—often when you are asleep or on the freeway.

Not knowing just *when* Time will occur makes it very difficult to plan your day.

Time also comes in different sizes. Normal people find that time arrives in nice big chunks, like a Gouda cheese. You can do any number of wonderful things with a whole chunk of cheese. *Your* time, however, most likely arrives in the form of rabbit pellets or baby peas, three at a time.

No wonder you're inefficient.

FINDING THE TIME

PLAYING HIDE-AND-SEEK WITH THE COSMOS

"If only I could find the time!" you wail.

Not likely. You have a better chance of finding Michael Bolton in your shower.

Time, you see, was created by the same team of engineers who made the Stealth bomber, and is therefore extremely sneaky. Although you may pride yourself on your skills in tracking down AWOL Fisher-Price people in the dead of night, using only the keen sensitivities of your bare feet, you're not likely to have such luck with Time.

Experts tell us to look for Time in unexpected places. That's because the experts have already looked in the logical places, like Times Square.

You could try poking into diaper pails or boarded up brothels, but you might as well just relax and have a piña colada, because Time is a really, really good hider, with a bazillion disguises and infinite patience to wait you out. It has apparently learned all the good hiding places from people like Jimmy Hoffa and Amelia Earhart.

SAVING TIME

Unfortunately, you can't save up your little pea-sized pieces of time to get one big useful chunk. Even if you wrap them in foil and stash them in the fridge, they'll just shrivel up and disappear like the rest of the scraps you've hidden in there.

You could try to put them up your nose just to amuse yourself.

There are, however, annoying little people with pocket protectors and eczema who want to tell you how to Save Time. Actually, what they really want to do is *sell* you this information in the form of a self-published book or a seminar in the church basement. You can listen politely if you wish, but it's not necessary, because they are all nuts and you'll save time just by not listening to them.

THE MYTH OF TIME MANAGEMENT

The Domestically Gifted will sniff that it's all a question of *Time Management*. Right. Easy for them to say; their time is already pretty well premanaged, coming as it does in chunks on such a regular basis, day after day, hour after hour, just like clockwork.

However, among people like yourself, for whom Time arrives in sporadic bursts, managing an entire dimension of the universe is a tad bit ambitious. Starting out on a smaller scale is advisable; for right now, it's sufficient that you manage your foot odor and that embarrassing static cling.

Besides, no matter what you do, Time goes blithely about its own business (which pretty much consists of ticking off seconds and scurrying from hiding place to hiding place) wholly unaffected by your officious efforts to get it to do anything other than tick and hide.

Time Management is, in fact, a euphemism for Time Charting, wherein you record everything you do in little boxes in an obscenely expensive book. Admittedly, this is helpful should you need to provide documentation to local arson investigators of your whereabouts on the night of September 12 at 6:47 P.M. when that mysterious fire broke out at the aerobics studio. However, it's of little use in Time Management, since after you get done writing everything down in that book, it's time to go to bed.

WHERE DOES TIME GO?

Not only does Time hide, it just up and leaves as soon as it arrives—a rude guest who drops in for a beer and to use the bathroom. Then *poof!* Gone. That's all she wrote. Arrivederci, baby.

To make matters worse, Time has a way of erasing itself from our memories. Many of you, finding yourself at the end of a day staring at the breakfast dishes, wonder if perhaps this missing block of time was caused by an alien abduction, wherein you were taken off to the mother ship where they performed horrifying medical experiments such as implanting cottage cheese in your thighs.

That is, in fact, exactly what happened. Of course, it makes perfect sense and explains why the laundry is never done. This never happens to the Domestically Gifted, since aliens (being intellectually and technically superior life forms) do not waste their time studying creatures who wax their garage floors and sanitize their oven dials.

ADAPTING TO TIME WARPS

So how does one deal with this cosmic short shrift in the allocation of time? Adaptability.

The key to the survival of any species is its ability to adapt to adverse situations, altering its behavior to accommodate nature's perverse sense of humor. Look at the kangaroo. After enduring centuries of cruel taunting for its huge feet, big ears, and bouncy gait, it developed kick-boxing skills to beat the tar out of the Aussies.

So what you need to do is turn to your own strengths and talents and see how they can be employed in offsetting your lack of time. Using the kangaroo as an example, you might want to sharpen your own kick-boxing techniques so you can beat the crap out of anyone who comments about how little you got done today.

THREE STEPS TO ORGANIZING YOUR LIFE

There are only three things you have to do if you want to get your life organized:

1. Write everything down.

2. Remember where you wrote it down.

3. Remember to remember Numbers 1 & 2.

Everybody knows that you have to write stuff down if you want to be organized. However, Domestically Gifted people have the uncanny ability to *remember* where they put these notes after they write them, and to actually find them later—a subtlety of the system that Domestically Impaired individuals such as yourself have not quite grasped.

THE SYSTEM—A WAY OF LIFE

So the first thing you have to do is get a System. A System is a fat book with lots of tabs and calendar-type organizational-looking stuff into which you write *EVERYTHING*. It will have a name that sounds like a running shoe and weigh slightly more than a large leg of lamb. You can find it in the aforementioned church basement seminars, or you can book a flight to Hong Kong and tear the response card out of the back of the airline magazine. In order to pay for this System, you will need a home equity loan.

The key to these Systems is that you write everything down in *one* place instead of having stuff strewn everywhere on Post-it Notes, matchbooks, and telephone disconnect notices. (Organized people, you see, do not jot down Important Appointments on the back of dry cleaning tickets.)

Until your System arrives in the mail, you can write everything down in the dust on the coffee table, since that is likely to remain undisturbed for months.

MAKING LISTS

A REWARDING SUBSTITUTE FOR ACTUAL WORK

Writing things down serves two purposes: One, you won't forget to do them; two, it's enormously satisfying to cross things off your list. Unfortunately, it is also enormously depressing to see only two things crossed off a thirty-item list.

So what you need to do is write down as much

stuff as possible that you *know* you're going to do, thusly:

1. Get up.

2. Go to the bathroom.

3. Flush toilet.

4. Pull up your panties.

5. Wash hands.

See? Five things to cross off your list first thing in the morning! And don't let anyone tell you that these things aren't important! If these things aren't Things to Do Today, well, what is?

Take Number 4 for example. What if you didn't pull up your panties? All manner of unpleasant things could occur if you were hobbling around all day with underwear around your ankles. If you had to go shopping, it would be almost impossible to get off the escalator or try on shoes.

Now keep adding to that list until you have about 800 Things to Do Today. Then prioritize them with the letters *A*, *B*, and *C*. Do not do the *C*'s, since they are low priority. Late in the day, change all the undone *B*'s into *C*'s.

Note: Be sure to use an opaque black felt-tip marker to cross off the items so nobody can actually read them, but will see the lengthy, impressive list you've managed to tackle. Have it dangling from your limp hand while you're collapsed on the couch.

19
Time Bandits
Safeguarding Your Time

INTERRUPTIONS

You would, of course, have far fewer problems with Time Management were it not for Interruptions. It's easier to handle interruptions once you know their true nature. *Important:* Interruptions are, in fact, nothing more than *other people trying to pawn off* their *to-do list on you.*

You must learn how to repel these people.

TELEPHONE SOLICITORS

Those annoying telephone solicitors can take a big chunk out of your day, particularly if you listen to their entire spiel, which will be read to you from a script the size of the Manhattan phone book by people whose oral reading skills are challenged by the McDonald's drive-thru menu.

These scripts usually start out with, "Hello, Mrs. Brown. How are you today?" This is an attempt to sound sincere. However, it can be safely assumed that anyone who calls you by your mother-in-law's name does not have a deep abiding interest in the state of your health. It is a good tip-off for you that this call is From A Stranger, since none of your friends would be foolhardy enough to ask such an open-ended question.

So the best thing to do is nip this call in the bud.

Here are some effective responses for when the caller asks, "How are *you* today?"

• "Well, I won't know for sure until the tests are back, but they think they might be able to save one of my legs."

• "Oh, I'm so glad you asked! Honey, you would not *believe* how heavy my flow is today. . . . I've been through five super plus *and* backup pads this morning, if you can believe it. . . . And the *cramps* . . . whooooaaaaah!"

• "I'm much better now, thank you, since the acquittal."

• (snapping) "Oh, sure! *Now* you ask. Where were you YESTERDAY when I was all by myself on my BIRTHDAY, sitting there in the DARK with just that lousy CUPCAKE with ONE LOUSY CANDLE and fresh out of PROZAC."

• (sweetly) "How lovely of you to ask! Why, I'm just wonderful! The birds are tweeting, the sun is shining, and my daffodils have poked their perky little yellow heads up from the ground, and well . . . I just haven't felt this giddy since Franklin Roosevelt slipped his hand up my dress."

The majority of callers will simply hang up. End of conversation. Back to what you were doing. Some, however, will not hear what you've just said, due to the fact that they weren't listening, and trip right on into the next phase of their pitch.

At this point, you can either hang up or employ one of the following techniques:

• Tell them to hang on while you go get a pen. Put the phone down and drive to the mall. Be sure to buy a pen while you're there.

• Decline any request for a donation or purchase on religious grounds, e.g., "I'm sorry, but lightbulbs are against my religion."

• Tell them that your son handles all business transactions for you, at which point you hand the phone to your toddler and whisper, "Do you want to talk to Big Bird?"

• Respond to any questions asked of you with a totally inappropriate answer. For example, if the caller asks, "Can we count on you for your support," say, "The calla lilies are in bloom again." Or when asked when would be a convenient time for an appointment, reply, "Barometer falling, southeasterly winds gusting to 40 miles per hour. Incoming! Incoming!"

Here are some sample scenarios:

• When the Kidney Association asks for a donation, tell them simply but firmly that you're using both kidneys at this time, and you consider the request highly presumptuous.

• Magazine subscription hucksters can be stopped in their tracks by asking them for a precise chemical analysis of the printing ink used in these magazines. Insist on documentation that the billithium count does not exceed .00215 microcosms per column inch.

• Carpet cleaners who "happen to be working in your area" should be told that you would be delighted to have them over on Tuesday, at which time they could hear your 90-minute presentation of an exciting new business opportunity with Amway.

• Requests for donations to spurious groups you have never heard of should be met with a businesslike "Thank you for returning my call in response to the Attorney General's Cease and Desist Order Number 43526."

• Enthusiastic hucksters informing you that you have *definitely* been named the recipient of one of the following three fabulous awards can be told, "Great! This is fantastic! Let me put you on the speaker phone so the entire law office can hear the good news."

Sometimes solicitors will attempt a form of courtesy by asking, "Is this a good time for you?" Your response should be:

• "Da, comrade. The lines are secure. All hail the motherland."

• "Yeah . . . just a minute . . . if you can hang on just a second . . . the coroner needs another trash bag."

• "Can't talk right now. The bankruptcy lawyer is here."

TELEPHONE CALLS FROM FRIENDS AND RELATIVES WHO JUST WANT TO *CHAT*

A telephone answering machine allows you to screen incoming calls and is the slickest way around Great-Aunt Sadie's hourly hiatal hernia update. Unfortunately, since you can't tell her you never got the message, you're obligated to call her back eventually or risk being cut out of the will.

There is a way around this, however. First, you let the machine screen the call. Once it's evident that the call is not from the state lottery office or Kevin Costner, you immediately press the numbers on your Touch-Tone phone, two or three at a time, for the next 20 seconds, then hang up. This will produce an incredibly annoying simulation of an answering machine in the last stages of its death throes.

When you see Aunt Sadie next Christmas, tell her how concerned you've been about her hernia, and you do *so* wish she'd keep in touch more often.

If you don't have an answering machine, keep a tape recorder handy on which you have prerecorded the various sounds of the doorbell, breaking glass, screaming children, the smoke alarm, and, for extreme cases, gunfire.

DROP-IN VISITORS

Your first line of defense against drop-in visitors is a solid door with no windows and a wide-angle peephole viewer. Interestingly, door peepholes were not originally designed as a security measure. Rather, they were invented by a woman in Pittsburgh, after moving

into a neighborhood composed of people selling mul-
tilevel marketing distributorships.

Pretending you're not home is a time-honored
ruse. To pull this off, you should have heavy draperies
at all the windows so they cannot peer in and see that
you *are* home lip-synching "Good Golly, Miss Molly"
into a vibrator.

Of course, the lack of sunlight is a little hard on
the houseplants, and you may find your pupils dilating
to alarming proportions, but life is full of little trade-
offs.

You can also hang signs up on the door—PLEASE
DO NOT RING BELL. BABY NAPPING. Of course, they
will want to knock on the door, so you should also post
a sign saying WET PAINT.

If, despite your best efforts, you get caught and
absolutely must answer the door, peek your head
through the crack and say, "I'd love to have you in, but
I've got a lower GI series at the doc tomorrow, and I'm
busy 'cleaning things out' if you know what I mean.
Uh-oh. Gotta run. . . ."

GOOD INTERRUPTIONS

- Husbands who suggest you're working too hard and
  really deserve a foot massage and some Godiva
  chocolates

- Children who want to show you how well they
  cleaned up their rooms

- The *Publisher's Clearinghouse* Prize Patrol

None of the above will ever happen in your life-
time.

CLUTTER

INVASION OF THE SANITY SNATCHERS

Clutter is not only unsightly, it is also one of the biggest time stealers, requiring hours on end each day just to shuffle it around into different piles and look for the Useful Stuff hidden underneath it, like your car keys and your diaphragm.

There are two different kinds of Clutter—Genuine and Mutated.

Genuine Clutter is stuff that is useless or ugly or both, no matter where it is—such as expired supermarket fliers, dead batteries, or anything obtained from a catalog that offers glitter pens and nose-hair clippers. In the event of your untimely demise, this is the stuff your friends and relatives will be sorting through, making weird faces and wondering aloud just what possessed you to keep that stuff.

Examples:

• Dried-up Magic Markers and moist towelettes

• 212 pieces of a 1,000-piece jigsaw puzzle

• Plastic bags full of candle-wax scrapings

• Collect-and-win game pieces from 1983

• Broken plastic whistles

• Unraveled eight-track tapes of Zamfir and the Haunting Melodies of His Pan Flute

Mutated Clutter is useful or attractive stuff that's hanging around where it doesn't belong. These items undergo a metamorphosis when moved out of their natural habitat, mutating into *clutter*. A sweat sock on your son's foot is clothing; on the kitchen counter, it is clutter.

Examples:

- Soy sauce packets in the medicine chest
- Paper clips in the soap dish
- Toggle bolts on the dresser
- Teenage Mutant Ninja Turtle action figures in the vegetable crisper
- Swimmer's nose clips in the silverware drawer

CLUTTER MAGNETS

In every home there exists a place where the molecular convergence of interplanetary gravitational electrons creates a concentrated magnetic pull on all clutter from a five-county area. This place is almost always the most highly visible and irritating location, such as the kitchen table.

Scientists have captured on film, in time-lapse infrared photography of the sort used on night-blooming cactuses, this amazing process. Items are sucked from toolboxes, purses, gym bags, glove compartments, and erector sets and, along with items that have flown off the back of open U-Haul trailers belonging to itinerant carnival workers, are deposited about your kitchen while you sleep.

This is why you will always have a collection of rusted plumbing washers, random dominoes and Candyland pieces, barrettes, arcade game tokens, bingo markers, Chap Stick, vegetable seed packets, pop beads, and fishing lures on your table.

CLUTTER STRATEGIES

TO DREAM THE IMPOSSIBLE DREAM

Handling Genuine Clutter requires only a trash bag and the ruthlessness of an IRS auditor-turned-serial-killer. You will need to muster the strength to resist imagining how valuable those broken shower curtain rings will be some day and envisioning the 1,001 Useful Things You Can Do with dismembered plastic dolls. *Do not read craft magazines before attempting to declutter!!*

The best way to rid yourself of Genuine Clutter is to pretend that Mel Gibson and Tom Selleck will be coming to your home tomorrow and they are *very* turned on by tidiness.

Of course, if after much agonizing you should decide to throw out that unidentified rubbery round black thing that's been lying in the spoon rest for 10 years, you will be informed, within the next 24 hours, that it was, in fact, an O-ring from the Space Shuttle and is worth 1.2 billion dollars.

Mutated Clutter, on the other hand, behaves much like antibiotic-resistant bacteria. You continue to attack it, but it keeps cropping up in different forms, stronger and more impervious to your efforts to eradicate it.

It procreates like zucchini in the middle of the

night; the pile of Legos in your child's room will undergo rapid cell division and send out runners underneath the carpet, then crop up in 133 different locations, many of which will not be apparent until you are walking barefoot carrying a hot cup of coffee.

You *could* handle Mutated Clutter by putting everything back where it came from. It will then mutate back into Useful, Attractive Stuff—sort of a domestic alchemy.

But that's *way* too much work. And the results are about as lasting as a Clinton promise.

Instead, change your definition of what belongs where. Express annoyance when the dog brush isn't on the sofa where you can find it. Keep the toilet paper in the liquor cabinet. When your husband asks you where his golf tees are, say, "Why, they're in the washing machine where they belong, dear." Soon, just to annoy you, he'll start leaving them in other places—like in his golf bag.

IF YOU COULD KEEP TIME IN A BOTTLE, IT WOULD BE A URINE SPECIMEN

HOW TO PIDDLE AWAY A DAY

The amazing thing about being Domestically Impaired is the ability to stay constantly busy while accomplishing nothing. Very few of you actually lounge around Doing Nothing. That would be boring. The key is the ability to Do Nothing while Appearing to Do Something.

For Example: It starts out innocently enough. You

have every good intention of cleaning out the hall closet. You gather your boxes and trash bags and head purposefully toward the task at hand, feeling quite smug in your resolve, and rather like one of those TV commercial housewives.

Except those TV commercial housewives wear designer chambray workshirts and full make-up, while you're wearing torn sweats, corn pads, and Blistex. Knowing that to do a proper job you need the proper tools, you head upstairs to wardrobe and make-up. An hour later, dressed and groomed, you descend the stairs, ready to tackle that closet.

But first, you'd better make some coffee. You'll want some for a relaxing, well-deserved break when you're through. But you really ought to have some of that European kind, don't you think? Such occasions call for beverages with names like Suisse Vienna Mocha Vanilla Creme de Cappuccino Amaretto Menthe. Well, you needed to go to the store anyway.

But as long as you're going, you might as well pick up a few other things you've been meaning to get.

And, being the frugal and incredibly efficient homemaker you pretend you are, you decided to take along your cents-off coupons. Unfortunately, you haven't had a chance to clip any lately, so you begin to sort through papers dating back to the Kennedy administration.

Then, of course, you get interested in the articles (you've been meaning to read about that Desert Storm thing everybody was talking about), at which point you realize it is now after lunchtime. Since there really isn't anything handy to eat, and you were going to the store anyway, you decide to pick up a burger at a drive-thru.

Being health-conscious, you remember an article in a magazine somewhere that listed the fat and nutritional content of each of the menu items at the various fast-food restaurants. You spend the next two hours paging through the last six months of women's magazines.

You now know 17 ways to perk up your love life while your husband's out of town, how to julienne carrots while nursing a baby, and how to safely incubate snake eggs in your microwave.

Unable to find the fast-food article, you grab a handful of Oreos, a jar of Cheez Whiz, and a spoon and wolf down lunch in front of the TV while watching a bald woman who looks like Arnold Schwarzenegger in a tube top lecture you on nutrition. You shake your head and lament your lack of time for normal meals.

At that point, you get a phone call reminding you that the church meeting is at your house in 20 minutes. You shovel up all the newspapers, coupons, and magazines and stuff them into a box in the front hall closet, then collapse into a chair after your hard day.

Moral of the story: Women with time on their hands just aren't washing thoroughly.

20
Conclusion
I'm OK, You're OK, and the House Is a Pit

There are cobwebs on the ceiling
And mud prints in the halls;
I'm cultivating mushrooms
In bathroom shower stalls.

My mending basket overflows
With clothes aged out of style;
I get my daily exercise
Climbing laundry piles.

The home-baked cookies come from elves
Who live in hollow trees;
The carpet needs a good shampoo;
The dog, alas, has fleas.

You can't eat off my kitchen floor
(There's plates we use for that);
The coffee's fresh, the cups are clean;
I'd rather laugh and chat.

Though some may sneer and criticize
My home's casual interior,
I'm glad to live the way I do
So *they* can feel superior.